Crime Prevention in Schools:
specification, installation and maintenance of intruder alarm systems

Department of Education and Science

Building Bulletin 69

London: Her Majesty's Stationery Office

i

364.4
EDu

FOREWORD

In recent years there has been a considerable increase in the use of expensive equipment such as micro computers and video recorders in our schools. This has made many schools more susceptible to incidents of break-ins and theft. Intruder alarm systems have an important role to play in preventing crimes of this nature in schools. This Building Bulletin offers practical advice on the selection, installation and use of intruder alarm systems. The bulletin complements the other initiatives I am taking in cooperation with local education authorities, teachers and governors to make our schools more secure.

John Butcher MP
Parliamentary Under-Secretary of State

Contents

Acknowledgements

Research was carried out by the Architects and Building Branch of the Department of Education and Science. The Department would like to thank the LEAs that gave access to their schools and details of their experience of installing and managing intruder alarm systems. Thanks are also due to SCEME (Society of Chief Electrical and Mechanical Engineers), Crime Prevention Centre and Home Office for their very useful comments and observations during production of this bulletin. Technical literature and comment were provided by many companies in the security industry and the Department is grateful for this very valuable support to our research.

The project team members were:

Superintending Architect:	A J Branton
Principal Engineer:	M J Patel
Senior Engineer:	R M Heard
Editor:	A Haworth-Roberts
Graphics Designer:	H Omar

1 Introduction

1. The incidence of theft and vandalism in schools, has steadily increased during the last decade. In England, during 1985, crimes of this nature amounted to losses of approximately £30 million. In human terms there can be a very serious impact upon the morale of pupils, teachers and parents.

2. Schools are particularly vulnerable since they are generally open to wide sections of the community, have elevations hidden from public view and increasingly contain valuable electronic equipment. Expensive portable items like computers, televisions, videos, tape recorders, keyboards etc, are easily stolen and disposed of.

3. Coordinated with other security measures intruder alarms can be cost effective in combatting crime in schools. Local Education Authorities (LEAs) have employed intruder alarms with varying degrees of success in terms of technical effectiveness and value for money. Typically, LEAs commenced by installing a few systems on an ad-hoc basis and many now embark upon major capital programmes to install alarms in many educational buildings.

4. LEAs have evolved their own policies for the installation, maintenance and management of intruder alarm systems. As the number of systems increases and technology advances, there is a need for LEAs to consider their policies, and make changes where advantages can be identified. The purpose of this Bulletin is to provide guidance on the management and technical aspects of forming policies for installing and operating intruder alarm systems in educational buildings. Part 7 shows examples of good practice based upon case studies. Appendices 1-6 contain the technical details of intruder alarm systems.

2 Intruder alarm systems

5. Schools can be subject to a variety of different acts of vandalism and break-ins. *BB* 67[1] suggests that measures like:

- clear management policy
- prompt repairs
- involvement of local community

can all help in reducing the number of break-ins.

6. However, there will always be some schools in any LEA where in spite of the above actions the break-ins and thefts will persist. In such cases the installation of an intruder alarm system may be the only answer. Intruder alarm systems, if correctly installed and used, can be highly effective in combating crime. Table 1 shows the effect of installing intruder alarm systems in 15 schools in an LEA in the North of England. As indicated there were 119 break-ins in the 15 schools for the year preceding the installation of an intruder alarm system. After two years the annual number of break-ins had reduced to 13.

7. In 1986 school buildings in Great Britain suffered fire damage in excess of £30m. Fire alarm and detection systems can clearly help to reduce this loss. However, in the absence of an automatic fire detection system, there is considerable benefit in having a well designed intruder alarm system, as it can activate an alarm in response to the effects of a fire. Also since arsonists are often intruders as well, the alarm system may either deter an arsonist or activate an alarm before a fire has been started.[2]

---

[1] DES *Building Bulletin No 67 Crime Prevention in Schools – Practical Guidance*, published in 1987. Details various preventative measures against vandalism, theft and arson in schools.

[2] DES is currently preparing separate guidance on technical aspects of firealarm systems. Topics to be covered include fire detectors, system design, operation and communication links.

Effectiveness

8. Intruder alarm systems if they are to operate satisfactorily must be:

- correctly designed
- properly installed
- sensibly used
- regularly maintained

9. If any of the above actions is neglected the system will be prone to false alarms or, worse still fail to operate at a critical time. False alarms which require call-outs can prove to be very expensive. Some of the earlier systems were particularly susceptible to false alarms, which resulted in loss of credibility of intruder alarm systems generally. However, a modern system based on microprocessor controls, central monitoring and improved detection technology can offer an excellent protection to any school. The appendices to this publication detail the technical considerations involved in selecting equipment and communication services.

Typical system

10. A typical school intruder alarm system will consist of movement detectors, a control panel and an audible alarm. In most cases a telephone line is used to automatically convey the alarm signal to the emergency telephone operator or alternatively to a private monitoring station so that the police can be alerted. In response, it is normal for the police to issue a radio message to despatch a patrol car to the scene of the alarm. Figure 1 illustrates a typical intruder alarm system and communication network.

TABLE 1.

History of break-ins at 15 north of England schools		
No. of break-ins in the year before the installation of an intruder alarm system.	No. of break-ins after intruder alarm system installation.	
	1st Year	2nd Year
119	43	13

Fig. 1   A typical intruder alarm system.

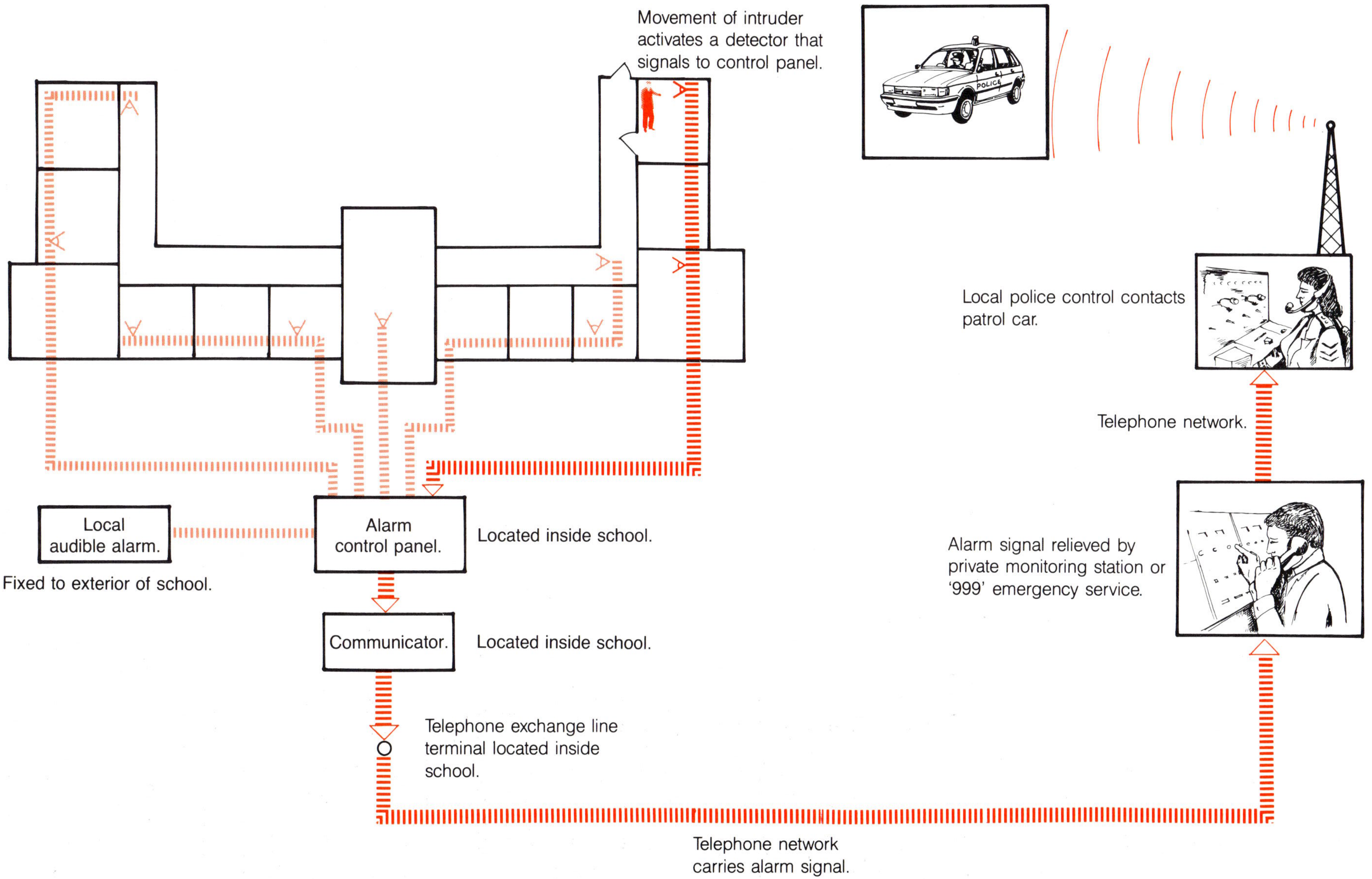

Movement of intruder activates a detector that signals to control panel.

Local police control contacts patrol car.

Telephone network.

Alarm signal relieved by private monitoring station or '999' emergency service.

Telephone network carries alarm signal.

Alarm control panel.

Located inside school.

Communicator.

Located inside school.

Telephone exchange line terminal located inside school.

Local audible alarm.

Fixed to exterior of school.

3

11. The large range of detectors includes devices that sense movement within the volume of space and more simple devices that sense opening doors or foot pressure. These days electronic movement detectors are the most widely used form of intruder detection. The passive infrared movement detector is fixed to a wall or ceiling and aimed into the space under protection. When an intruder moves in the space a change occurs in the infrared radiation received by the detector resulting in an alarm signal being sent to the control panel. Ultrasonic detectors use high frequency sound to detect movement by responding to changes in reflected sound waves caused by human movement. Similarly, microwave detectors use radio waves to sense movement. The detectors are connected to a control panel by cables similar to that used for telephone installations.

12. Modern control panels contain a good deal of complex electronic circuitry but are designed to be user-friendly, and may be simply operated by the layman. They can be used to switch 'on' and 'off' the entire system or selected parts of the system. Under normal circumstances an intruder alarm system is never switched off. When in 'off' mode it will still raise a local alarm if the system equipment or wiring is tampered with.

13. Many of the alarm companies and some LEAs operate central monitoring stations. Using a telephone line and a digital dialler connected to the alarm control panel the monitoring station is informed of alarm conditions. Most often the monitoring service extends to logging all events such as opening and closing times and may even advise the personal ID code used by the person operating the control panel. Although central monitoring imposes greater revenue costs it is gradually superseding the "999" automatic dialler and is generally preferred by most local police forces, who regard intruder alarm systems connected to central monitoring services as being more reliable, and less prone to false alarms.

14. Recently radio-operated alarms of reasonable quality have been developed. They may be useful in buildings where special problems impede conventional wiring such as the presence of asbestos. However they have a limited application particularly in large buildings.

15. Portable alarms consist of a single unit combining a detector, controls and audible alarm. They may be useful as a temporary measure to scare off the casual intruder but are unreliable and tend to become damaged or stolen by the more experienced intruder.

16. An intruder alarm system will only operate correctly if each component performs reliably.

Hence, only components of good quality should be used. The temptation to use low-priced, poor quality materials should be resisted. In extreme cases selection of inadequate components can lead to intruders passing undetected, high levels of false alarms and associated resetting charges.

17. Apart from ensuring quality of installation, LEAs also need policies which will achieve consistent designs, maintenance standardisation, and adequate user procedures. Many LEAs have realised the advantages of specifying an approved list of components, thus tenders from installing companies can be evaluated on a more equal basis. Similarly such standardisation holds maintenance advantages. Unless LEAs have a planned approach they can end up with different types of systems and high maintenance and resetting charges.

3 A planned approach

18. The design of an intruder alarm system must meet the requirements of the particular school and its problems.

19. There is very great value in looking at historical data. Records of break-ins, theft and arson attempts with the monetary value of loss can be vital in directing the application of finite resources into new alarm installations. Of similar importance is the need for continuing monitoring to quantify the benefit of installed intruder alarms. This helps to evaluate the effectiveness of different types of intruder alarm systems and components. Analysis can enhance the quality of future policies for design and installation. Geographical trends are another relevant factor. One way to determine whether an intruder alarm system should be installed or not is to carry out a Risk Assessment Audit. Building Bulletin 67 deals with Risk Assessment methodology in detail. Schools that are identified as above average risk should be given high priority for the installation of an intruder alarm system. Analysis may reveal that protecting one high risk site simply changes another nearby low risk site into a high risk site. Hence, in some situations it may be decided, with foresight, to simultaneously protect all relevant premises that lie within close proximity of each other.

20. To evaluate design and monitor the schemes' effectiveness LEAs should set up liaison groups on intruder alarm systems. This group may typically comprise representatives from the Education Department, Treasurer's Department, Property Services, LEA's insurance company and the local police force. A typical example is in the north of England, where the LEAs of Durham County, Cleveland and Northumberland have coordinated their efforts to form the North East Regional Schools Security Group and have benefited from a united approach against crime in schools. Cheshire has done much on risk management that has also proved useful to other authorities. Common problems exist throughout the country and local security liaison groups may gainfully establish communication links between themselves. Re-inventing the wheel is to no one's benefit.

Planning policy

21. This section deals with the many technical and administrative functions that need to be taken account of by LEAs in determining a policy for installing and owning intruder alarm systems. As owners of multiple alarm installations, LEAs need to develop policies that will enable them to move with the times and achieve cost effectiveness.

22. In 1988 it typically cost approximately £1,000 and £3,000 to install a basic intruder alarm system in a primary and secondary school respectively. For an average school the maintenance costs, excluding call-outs and repairs, may typically be £150 per year whilst central station monitoring could cost a further £75. Clearly intruder alarm systems are expensive to install and maintain. LEAs should undertake a rolling programme of installations in schools with high instances of break-ins.

23. It is important that LEAs are not constrained either technically or contractually from obtaining competitively priced intruder alarm services. This is achievable by building into their policy: freedom of choice for determining purveyors of installations; maintenance service, and central station monitoring. Essentially the policy must formalise the process for intruder alarm installation, maintenance and monitoring. The LEA's own administrative function of intruder alarm management should be an integral part of an overall policy.

24. The LEA's administration must be tailored to their policies for designing, installing, maintaining, and monitoring alarm systems. Cost control is most vital. The nature of intruder alarms can produce numerous invoices in respect of engineers' visits to reset or repair alarm systems. Often, the work is carried out in response to an automatic alarm signal and the owner of the alarm system has little opportunity to control or supervise the work. Invoice sums may be relatively small but the cumulative effect can be very substantial. The temptation to "routinely" authorise such small invoices for payment should be resisted. Manual or computerised data analysis should be used to highlight the number of invoices and accumulative monetary value relative to any alarm system. Anomalies can therefore be investigated resulting in appropriate remedial action. Detailed cost assessment can reflect upon the quality of alarm installations and servicing. Comparisons may be made between different installers and servicing organisations. In some cases changes in the pattern of building use or staff can be identified as a reason for cost fluctuations.

25. It is reasonably straightforward to budget for recurring charges for maintenance and monitoring. Similarly, a budget can be established to fund a rolling programme of new installations and additions to existing installations.

Installation policy

26. The competitive tendering of new installation works or the modification to existing systems will, by definition, ensure value for money. However, it is essential to seek tenders against a full client specification. Failure to specify contractual and technical standards invites competing companies to produce the lowest quotation based upon their own contract conditions and minimal technical standards. Only full specification ensures that tenders can be assessed on a fully comparative basis. Similarly, close supervision may be necessary to ensure compliance with specification.

27. Production of a list of standardised selected components and installation methods and use of appropriate contract conditions will enable existing installations to be extended by open competition. This is a vital consideration, since most basic installations will require extending, often to a value of work exceeding the original installation cost. It would therefore be commercially inappropriate to be contractually tied to the original installers of individual alarm installations. The policy for owning and operating intruder alarm systems, may advantageously facilitate options for the future, permitting any selected private contractor or suitably trained direct labour work force to implement adaptations to any individual installation.

28. Many LEAs have benefited from being committed to a standard specification. Good quality components installed to a high standard make for a reliable installation. Inferior standards produce unacceptable levels of false alarms and are not cost effective. A short list of "standard" control panels aids user familiarity and further reduces false alarms. This also offers adavantages of future competitive tendering of maintenance and monitoring service.

Maintenance policy

29. Technically, as a minimum, the routine standard of maintenance should satisfy the requirements of BS 4737 Section 4.2. Owners of multiple alarm installations have a wide scope in formulating a policy for maintenance. Scope should exist within the policy to employ any selected

private contractor or trained direct labour force to perform routine or call-out service on any intruder alarm installation.

30. LEAs often invite tenders for various building services maintenance contracts. These services include heating, ventilation, air conditioning, electrical services, lifts, communication systems and fire alarms. There is no valid reason why intruder alarm maintenance should be excluded from competitive tendering. Typically the building stock could be divided into a number of groups with a different group being put out to tender each year, under a three year contract. Some proprietary systems, such as sound monitoring, can necessitate a tied maintenance agreement with the owners of the proprietary system. However, in all normal intruder alarm installations the specification of standard components and installation methods should offer complete flexibility for maintenance arrangements. As with other building services there is a commercial benefit in periodic re-tendering procedures.

31. Deciding upon the extent of the maintenance contract is a fairly complicated process. Historically, intruder alarm companies were content to set a price for a year's routine maintenance, but levy additional charges for ad hoc replacements and call-outs. Often the customer has been tied to the installing company's maintenance contract and suffered the expense of the business that unreliable alarm systems have generated for the companies engaged in maintenance activities.

32. In recent years the intruder alarm industry has been under increased pressure to improve standards of reliability. Combined with technological advances this has produced a new generation of components with enhanced immunity to false alarms. Accordingly reliable intruder alarm systems can now be installed. In respect of a newly completed installation employing modern technology, the industry is now more likely to direct the customer towards a fully comprehensive maintenance contract, in preference to the historic 'maintenance with repairs at additional cost' type. Trends will continue to evolve and the customer's maintenance policy needs to be flexible to readily adjust to the most advantageous method prevailing at any particular time. Depending upon the characteristics of different installations, it may be most viable for the customer to opt for both a fully comprehensive contract and repairs at extra charge type agreements, to suit any particular installation. When opting for a fully comprehensive arrangement it is essential that the customer's tender documents fully define the scope of the maintenance contract. Call-outs to a real intruder activation or user-induced false alarms may reasonably be charged at additional

cost. However, the tender documents should invite tenderers to state their rates for the type of call-out, call-out time of day and day of week in order to facilitate competitive comparison.

33. Where owners of multiple alarm installations have established a large portfolio of highly reliable standard alarm installations, it is probably most cost effective to invite tenders for the basic routine maintenance with call-out charges levied separately, in accordance with tendered schedule of rates.

34. The tender documents should include a maintenance specification, to meet as a minimum the requirements of BS 4737 Section 4.2. To facilitate multiple installation tendering a schedule should describe the apparatus at each protected premises. It is not recommended that the premises should be identified at an early tender stage since widespread knowledge of the protected buildings and hence the unprotected building stock creates a security exposure. The tender documents should invite tenderers to submit a schedule of rates for every conceivable repair or call-out function. The price for performing the basic routine maintenance should be separately detailed. It would be reasonable for quoted maintenance prices to hold firm for a 12 month period agreement with subsequently indexed linked fluctuations in the remaining years of the contract period.

Monitoring policy

35. Central station monitoring is not an absolute requirement for every intruder alarm installation. Local audible alarms together with a 999 auto-tape dialler may adequately meet the required level of security and be more cost effective. LEAs with large numbers of intruder alarm installations should have a clear policy for determining when central station monitoring is a justifiable requirement. Furthermore, the policy should define procedures for obtaining the required level of monitoring and also retain contractual freedom for future changes to enhance monitoring facilities or move to more competitive terms. Where large numbers of intruder alarm installations are owned, the viability of establishing an around the clock in-house central monitoring station should be evaluated. Central station costs have been saved in one southern county where the local fire service has agreed to receive the intruder alarm calls and subsequently alert the local police.

36. In determining the break even point at which an intruder alarm installation can be justifiably connected to a monitoring service, the service charges need to be evaluated against the level of security and usefulness of the monitoring facilities

provided. Appendix 6 of this publication "central monitoring stations" describes the stations' functions. Essentially, the required signalling between the premises and the central station provides a level of assurance that the alarm system is in operating order and that integrity exists in the alarm system communication links. This achieves a superior level of security to that attainable with the 999 auto-dialler, and exclusive telephone line arrangement. Additional benefits may enable the keyholder, in conjunction with the central station operator, to reset the system, following an alarm condition, thereby eliminating the need for an immediate service engineer's visit to reset the system. Many fault conditions can be automatically reported to the control station thereby ensuring prompt remedial action. If an alarm signalling attempt fails, further digital dialling attempts are made automatically and may include alternative telephone line routes. Monitored, direct, private wires increase levels of security further. Facilities for non-alarm data monitoring can record opening and closing events and the relevant user code identification. Fire alarms, lift alarms, heating, and other building services may be beneficially monitored. In particular, scope exists where the building stock contains automated services that may easily lend themselves to remote condition monitoring. In preparing a policy for using central monitoring services it is therefore, necessary to determine the usefulness of the facilities available.

37. Schools are of varying size and are located in greatly differing areas of risk. Small and medium sized schools in low risk areas may be most cost-effectively protected by an alarm system connected to a conventional 999 auto-tape dialler. Where a history of break-ins exists, or if fairly valuable property is *in situ,* the ordering of an exclusive ex-directory telephone line, connected to the 999 auto-tape dialler, should satisfactorily meet security requirements. Large schools and further education establishments increasingly contain computers and audio visual equipment and are usually a high risk. Accordingly, central station monitoring can normally be justified for this type of premises. Local education authorities need to assess the potential loss and risk applicable to any particular building. Therefore, the policy on central monitoring should be flexible to allow for the special needs of individual buildings.

38. To achieve future cost effectiveness, any central monitoring arrangement must contain the freedom of choice for future monitoring commitments. For the multiple user of central station facilities, benefit can be derived from tendering on a block system for the connection of a large number of intruder alarm systems to a monitoring service. Any contract or monitoring

agreement should respect this need to consider and respond to future options.

39. It may be possible for LEAs with a large number of intruder alarm systems to beneficially establish their own in-house central monitoring station. The savings in the recurring charges levied by monitoring contractors must be evaluated against the expenditure of establishing and maintaining an in-house monitoring station. The case for establishing an in-house station will to a large extent depend upon the geographical area of the LEA. Where the building stock is predominantly in areas that suffer from high crime rates and where the building stock has a history of theft and arson attacks it is likely that central station monitoring is justifiable. Accordingly, where monitoring is required for a significant number of premises, in-house monitoring should be considered. LEAs must assess their own break-even point at which in-house facilities become viable. The benefits of in-house monitoring include the facility to economically add every new alarm system to the monitoring station. Also, apparently low risk buildings can be cost-effectively monitored. Data storage methods provide a history of events for every building, including alarms, opening and closing times. In conjunction with appropriate software, alarm system maintenance and repair can be controlled and monitored. Additionally intruder alarm system administration and financial control can be incorporated in the software package to include the raising of orders and invoice authorisation.

40. The viability of in-house monitoring also depends upon the requirement for additional in-house staff resources to operate the monitoring station on a 24 hour rota. Some LEAs will already have a 24 hour security or emergency desk to which the monitoring terminal can be added. However, additional staff resources may still be needed to ensure an adequate level of VDU terminal supervision.

41. One LEA that operates its own central station has 250 intruder alarm systems monitored. Usefully, some other monitored items include lift alarms, sewage pump failure alarms, and building services such as low temperature alerts to warn of heating plant failure and thus prevent frost damage. In 1985 the monitoring equipment cost the authority £12,000 and in 1987 the annual comprehensive maintenance charge was approximately £1,200 which included regular software updating. The full software package provides for the efficient administration of all the LEA's alarm systems. Placed with external organisations, the LEA estimates that their annual monitoring charges would currently be in the order of £20,000. It is imperative that any proposal to establish an in-house monitoring station is fully assessed on the facts applying to the individual owner of multiple intruder alarm installations. In respect of this, liaison should be carried out with all interested parties, including the local police force. Fact-finding visits to existing users of in-house monitoring systems can be highly beneficial. The consequences of a system failure are extremely serious, therefore system reliability and good maintenance support are essential requirements.

4   Design of intruder alarm systems

42.   A well-designed intruder alarm system will satisfy the following basic essentials:

■ Provide early detection of the presence of an intruder or an attempt to gain unauthorised entry.

■ A tolerance of environmental background disturbance whilst providing high levels of detection sensitivity ensuring that false alarm factors are beyond the range of detection.

■ Effectively communicate alarm signals.

43.   Intruder alarm systems are a building services component. Other services, heating, lighting and ventilation are designed to a combination of statutory standards and recognised guidance documents.

44.   BS 4737 *Intruder Alarm Systems in Buildings* defines essential standards for the system its components, and their installation, but is not intended to provide guidance on the extent of any intruder alarm system. Parts of BS 4737 have been in the course of revision during the preparation of this publication. Readers are advised to refer to the latest available edition of BS 4737. Unlike other building services the designers of intruder alarm systems must determine for themselves the level of necessary security and the appropriate extent of individual alarm systems. Consultation with the local crime prevention officer can help in rationalising these considerations.

45.   The designer's prime function is to maximise the amount of protection against intruders from finite financial resources. Often, the designer possesses a list of non-alarmed buildings that are frequently the targets of theft and arson attacks. At the same time, protection may require extending at other buildings where the level of potential loss has increased.

46.   Increasingly, community use of schools imposes greater demands upon the flexibility of intruder alarm systems. In many cases there will be a long-term advantage in selecting a system that can be readily zoned to suit changes of occupancy patterns. This will enable unoccupied areas to be protected whilst other areas are in use.

47.   The design process involves the assessment of risks and determination of the optimum level of investment in security measures and then applying

the technology in intruder alarm systems with expert knowledge. DES *Building Bulletin 67 Crime Prevention in Schools − Practical Guidance* offers advice on reducing risks and also contains examples of risk analysis. However, in many practical situations, historical data will influence the allocation of financial resource expended in intruder alarm installations. In respect of this a system of data collection should identify the value of loss and the number of attacks upon the individual premises within the building stock. Effectiveness of different intruder alarm installations should be regularly evaluated thereby providing a valuable feedback to improve future design work.

Technical aspects

48.   It is recommended that LEAs should try to develop a common technical standard for all their schools rather than adopt a particular proprietary system. This makes available to the customer the benefits of competitive tendering. Detectors, controls and ancillary components should be defined by their performance specification or by an approved list of proprietary products. Almost certainly, an alarm system will require numerous additions and adaptations throughout its operational life. It is advantageous if the finished installation lends itself to future revisions by competitive tendering processes. In respect of this an intruder alarm installation can be as flexible as an electric lighting or power installation. Contractors may submit their own conditions stipulating that the alarm control panel and other essential parts of the installation will not constitute an outright sale, but will be supplied only on a rental agreement. Acceptance of these terms may prohibit competitive tendering for future alteration work.

49.   Components must be selected for their compatibility with their working environment. Temperature, humidity, radio signals, vibration, sunlight, air motion and passing vehicles are just a small number of the random factors that may stimulate a false alarm, or reduce the sensitivity of detection. Component selection may be aided by referring to the technical appendices contained herein describing each common form of detection against which manufacturers' specifications may be compared. It should therefore be possible for the designer to specify the type of detection technology and its required performance in terms of range,

sensitivity, and level of false alarm immunity. Alarm control panels and communication equipment are similarly described enabling the designer to consider the broad options.

50.   The quality of installation workmanship must be fully defined. Where the designer is responsible for a large building stock there is considerable advantage in producing a standard specification. BS 4737: Section 4.1 includes subsections specifically referring to the planning and installation of intruder alarm systems. However, it is still incumbent upon the designer to specify particular requirements. In the absence of a detailed technical specification and layout drawings, installers will use their own commercial judgement to determine installation standards. Typically, interconnecting cables may be simply clipped to the surface, enclosed in a lightweight conduit, trunking or laid in floors and ceilings. The cable routes chosen may be the most economic to the installer and not be fully sympathetic to the aesthetics of the building. The following list schedules appropriate items for consideration for inclusion in a standard specification:

- General conditions of contract and preliminaries

- Requirements for all materials to be used, including control panels, communicators, detectors, zone omit units, shunt locks, wiring, conduits, trunking and fixings

- Requirements for ordering telephone line connection and central monitoring station services

- Agreed procedures for informing the local police that the new alarm system is in operation

- Liaison with building user to determine appropriate first and final entry route

- Design considerations to comply with BS 4737 and where appropriate, the latest edition of the IEE Regulations for Electrical Installations.

  i   Define proposed cable routes and method of cable fixing throughout entire length of cable route. It is good design practice to ensure that the maximum system voltage drop does not exceed 1 volt between any two points, thereby ensuring detectors are working within design parameters. Generally, cables below a height of 2 metres require physical protection against mechanical damage.

  ii   Ascertain user's need for shunt lock, zone omit facilities and 24 hr protection where proprietary zone omit units may be necessary.

  iii   Prescribe the use of catenary wire to carry overhead alarm cables. Similarly, define minimum cable depth for underground routes and type of cable and protection to be employed. Cable joints shall be terminated in tamper resistant termination boxes.

  iv   Coordinate the provision and position of the new power supply to serve the alarm system. Comply with requirements to physically segregate alarm signal wires from mains voltage wiring.

  v   Define proposed position of detection devices, with drawings as necessary. Include the use of dummy bells, visible on all external elevations. For new works, coordinate a concealed conduit installation where feasible.

  vi   Make due allowance for the system to possess flexibility and be sympathetic to future changes, particularly in respect of changing patterns of occupancy.

- Provision of user instructions that are easy for the layman to understand. Also specify need for the installing company to educate users regarding the operation of the alarm system

- Installation tenderers to competitively submit details of their maintenance, central monitoring and call-out charges in respect of the alarm installation tendered for. Seek confirmation of the method for calculating future increases in these recurring service charges. Where required, state that it should be the customer's prerogative to terminate any maintenance or rental agreement by giving reasonable notice

- Specify that the system must be supplied on an outright ownership basis, unless the customer is fully prepared to accept the installing company's rental conditions

- Refer to the need for the compliance with the Health and Safety at Work Act and the statutory requirements applicable where asbestos is found to be present

51.   The above list is intended as a general guide from which the designer may tailor a particular specification.

Installation

52.   The designer's documents should not only detail technical component requirements but must also stipulate the standards of workmanship and method of installation. Basic standards vary between installing organisation and the individuals employed upon any particular project. It is therefore

incumbent upon the customer to clearly define requirements, within the tender documents and subsequently diligently supervise all stages of the installation work. Similarly, the personnel assigned to the installation should be of "good character" and respect the confidential nature of their activities.

53. The majority of intruder alarm installations are carried out by private contracting companies many of whom are on the National Supervisory Council for Intruder Alarms, (NSCIA), roll of approved installers. The NSCIA was established in 1971 with support from insurers and some of the larger companies involved in the installation of security alarm systems. As a non-profit making body, it has produced a code of practice for the design, installation, operation, maintenance and servicing of intruder alarms. The NSCIA operates an inspection board to implement its recommendations and maintain standards of workmanship. For installers to gain entry on the roll of approved installers they have to demonstrate conformity to a required standard of business management. Their completed installations and 365 days per year call-out service must comply with the requirements of BS 4737. The Electrical Contractors' Association (ECA) and the Electrical Contractors' Association of Scotland has formed a security group. A function of the group is to form a register of electrical contractors and security installers capable of installing, maintaining and supporting security systems to the requirements of British Standards(BS 4737 for intruder alarms). In conjunction with this a code of practice has been produced by the ECAs and a procedure for inspection has been established.

54. The British Security Industry Association (BSIA) comprises some of the largest manufacturers and installers of security systems. Its board based membership includes the fields of CCTV, guard and patrol services. It is a self-regulatory trade association that aims to advance standards in intruder alarm systems as well as the other security fields. All BSIA security system manufacturers and installers are required to comply with BS 4737 and BS 5750. A customer complaints procedure operates under which inspections are carried out.

55. Factors relating to the size of a company or its length of time in business may render many local companies and new enterprises unacceptable for inclusion upon a roll of approved installers. However, many of these developing companies can be competitive in producing work to a satisfactory standard in their effort to gain a share of the market. The Inspectors Approved Alarm Installers, (IAAI), has various membership categories, to complement companies of different size and capability. Guidance is offered to new or developing

companies, in meeting the requirements of the IAAI inspection process. Whichever course the customer follows it is wise to seek references and otherwise ascertain the standards of workmanship and service support relative to any individual company that is intended for inclusion on a tender list. In respect of this the local police force or relevent insurance company may advocate the use of alarm companies with membership of a trade body. However, for LEAs, statutory regulations may prevent the use of member only clauses in contracts. Before an installation is commenced the customer's supervisor, together with the installer's supervisor, should agree the extent and details of the work in principle. Accordingly, the installation process should be arranged to create the minimum of disruption to the normal business of the school premises.

56. Generally the designer's documents can only indicate the approximate location for detectors and exact positions may be mutually agreed on site to produce the most effective, false alarm resistant form of intruder protection. Intermediate inspections help to ensure compliance with the designer's requirements and also minimise the amount of any corrective work.

57. The installer should programme the work ensuring that any requirement to order a telephone line or liaise with the local police is arranged to suit the proposed commissioning date on the alarm installation. Similarly arrangements must be made to coordinate the provision of the mains power supplies and obtain user instructions and operating manuals, and where required, type-written "zone" location charts.

58. All components should be installed in a good workmanlike manner both in accordance with the related manufacturer's instructions and the requirements of BS 4737. Typical application requirements are detailed in the appendices for the different technologies of intruder detection. The process of site supervision should ensure that components are adequately fixed and that time-saving reliance placed upon adhesive fixings and masonry nails is not permitted where there is an advantage in providing a more permanent form of fixing. When mortice shunt switch locks are specified, the fitting should, preferably, be entrusted to a skilled locksmith or joiner.

59. Once the installer is satisfied the completed installation meets all requirements, the customer's supervisor should be invited to make a final inspection and if necessary produce a snagging list of defects and outstanding work. When the installation is fully to requirements commissioning should be carried out.

Commissioning

60.   Commissioning must ensure that all the interconnected components of an intruder alarm system operate within the parameters defined by the component manufacturers. To verify this requirement the appropriate form of test instrument should be used to quantify the electrical characteristics of the system and aid setting adjustments. Typically, breaking glass detectors and some forms of volumetric detection may be commissioned with the aid of proprietary commissioning equipment. More practical commissioning includes "walk testing" and other intruder simulation to aid detector sensitivity adjustments and confirm the effectiveness of the system to detect the presence of an intruder. In conjunction with this theoretical, out of range, walk testing and the deliberate operation of building services systems such as lighting, heating and ventilation should prove that the system possesses adequate immunity to environmentally induced false alarms. Where possible the commissioning environment should be similar to that prevailing during all periods when the alarm is armed. Unfortunately, not all environmental factors can be simulated, particularly weather variables. An experienced commissioning engineer will possess an ability to broadly assess the effects of such variables and compensate detection sensitivity settings accordingly. For example, some forms of volumetric detection are most sensitive when the air is still and the environment is cool.

61.   The various technologies of detection inherently have their own sensitivity or immunity to the whole range of environmental factors. Environmental factors can very often have a significant effect upon the sensitivity of the form of detection to real alarm conditions. This should be considered in conjunction with all of the prevailing environmental conditions at the time of commissioning.

62.   Digital communicators, 999 auto tape diallers or direct telephone lines should be tested under a simulated alarm condition. Where communication is extended to police it is imperative that testing methods fully comply with the requirements of the local police force. Digital communicators and direct lines are tested through to the central station. Only 999 Auto Diallers are tested through to the police.

63.   In some instances a local police force may request a time delay to precede the activation of the external audible alarm. The commissioning engineer should seek the customer's agreement of this proposal before implementation. Time delay may give vandals and arsonists opportunity to do extensive damage.

64.   Where local audible alarms create a nuisance legal action may be taken under the Control of Pollution Act 1974. As a precaution against such action and to reduce the likelihood of unnecessary noise it is desirable to automatically limit the sounding duration of an external audible alarm to a maximum period of 20 minutes. The local audible alarm should be auto-resetting, when the control panel is manually reset such that the alarm is ready to sound upon a subsequent activation. However, in remote locations or where there is a request for a longer duration of audible alarm an extension of the 20 minute period may not be contested by the local environmental health officer provided false alarm activations do not create a nuisance.

5 Maintenance of intruder alarm systems

65.   Increased levels of false alarms and failures to respond to the presence of intruders are typical symptoms of inadequately maintained intruder alarm systems. As with any other passive safety or security system there is a dependency upon a proper level of maintenance to ensure that the alarm system responds to a future emergency. BS 4737: Section 4.2. *Code of Practice for Maintenance and Records*, details requirements applicable to intruder alarm systems in buildings.

66.   There are two modes of maintenance, pro-active and reactive. In terms of value for money and optimum levels of security, planned, preventative maintenance increases system reliability, lowers false alarm rates, and minimises the waste of resources devoted to reactive maintenance in response to call-outs to attend to system faults and false alarms. Preventative maintenance visits can usefully be coordinated with a short period of user education thereby updating the keyholder's knowledge and educating new keyholders, with the consequential benefit of reduced levels of user-activated false alarms.

67.   Preventative maintenance works should be carried out to a written schedule at regular minimum intervals of six months for systems with remote signalling and annually for systems with local audible alarms only.

68.   The integrity of the customer's security must be respected at all times. Maintenance visits should be by prior appointment. The customer's on site representative is advised to check the identity credentials of all service personnel who in the course of their duty should be in possession of a current identity card, as issued by their employing organisation. Where it is proposed to test local audible alarms or remote signalling extended to the police, it is essential to adhere to procedures that have been previously agreed with the local police force. Similarly, the police should be advised of the operational status of any alarm installation and changes such as premises ownership, new keyholders and abandoned or removed installations. The quality of servicing personnel training and continued education is of prime importance. In respect of this, the customer should seek assurances from any prospective maintenance organisation. This education and training criterion equally applies to organisations who perform their own in-house installation and servicing functions.

69.   Security is an all-embracing concept and any single weakness can create a breach of total security. The building owner's maintenance regime should include non-alarm items such as doors, windows, fences and external security lighting

70.   The extent of the work required under the maintenance schedule is proportional to the size and technical complexity of the alarm system. Computerised and condition monitoring "intelligent" systems extend the basic maintenance schedule. Essentially, a visiting engineer will possess a computer-issued condition report directing the engineer to investigate and resolve reported conditions of near false alarm and possible deviation from the system's electronic parameters.

71.   A basic routine maintenance schdule includes the following items.

■   Instrumentation testing of detectors to verify conformity to technical parameters and consistency with previously recorded measurements.

■   Power supplies and voltage measurement at various system locations for conformity to detector operational parameters.

■   The satisfactory operation of detection devices and any necessary fine tuning of sensitivity adjustments.

■   Full visual inspection for physical damage, loose fixings, tampering evidence, or deterioration of flexible connections.

■   Condition testing of secondary batteries and replacement as necessary together with the routine replacement of systems employing dry cell batteries. Batteries utilised in wire-free alarm systems should be replaced in accordance with the equipment suppliers' recommendations and within the requirements of BS 6799.

■   Verification of the satisfactory operation of local audible alarms and the replacement of their integral, sealed, secondary batteries before the expiry of their rated service life expectancy.

■   The correct operation of auto-tape diallers, digital communicators and the communication medium.

■   The functioning of the entire combined alarm system throughout all its stages of interconnection.

In addition to the basic scheduled items detailed above, further tests should be carried out in accordance with the recommendations of equipment manufacturers, BS 4737, or any other appropriate codes of practice, as produced by individual maintenance companies or relevant trade associations.

72.   At any moment an alarm condition may be instigated by an intruder, environmental factor or a system fault. Also an anomaly in the system's condition may become apparent whilst the system is in the occupied, disarmed status, or when the setting procedure fails. In respect of these considerations it may be required at any time to reset automatic communication equipment and repair or isolate a faulty section of the alarm installation, thereby restoring the maximum amount of the intruder alarm system back into use. In the event of a false alarm activation every effort should be made to determine and hence eradicate the cause of the false alarm before re-arming the intruder alarm system and resetting any associated remote signalling apparatus. Where remote alarm signalling is extended to the police, resetting procedures should fully comply with local police force policy. BS 4737: Section 4.2 *Code of Practice for Maintenance and Records,* requires that remote signalling equipment should be reset by a member of the maintenance organisation's staff or by the coordinated efforts of the subscriber and central control station where this alternative method is appropriate. For schools it is usually the school keeper that fulfills the subscriber's role. British Standards require that the maintenance organisation should, under normal circumstances, reach the protected premises within 4 hours from the time of the request to attend. The maintenance organisation should establish and maintain a record log of maintenance and alarm events for each alarm system. Any written or computer records should be protected from unauthorised access.

73.   'Engineer reset' is an expression used within the alarm industry to imply that an activated alarm system is subsequently reset by an 'engineer' employee of an alarm maintenance company. Often, this task involves little more than pushing a button and confirming the reason for the alarm activation. Where a fault exists it is usually possible to operate the alarm control panel to restore most of the system and temporarily isolate only the failed section of the system. A full repair is then carried out during normal working hours. Some LEAs have found economic benefit in fulfilling this resetting role for themselves, since as owners of multiple alarm systems considerable costs can be incurred from contractors call-out charges. However, in most areas the agreement of the local police is necessary and is more likely to be forthcoming where the LEA can demonstrate competence in managing its alarm systems coupled with a low rate of false alarms.

74.   Owners of multiple intruder alarm installations are advised to retain their own records of maintenance and alarm activation for each individual system. Auditing methods may subsequently be used to identify troublesome alarm installations and effect remedial action. Such information may collectively reflect upon future design considerations and lists of approved installers. Furthermore when historical records are in the sole possession of an outside organisation, valuable data may be lost subsequent to changes following the future competitive tendering of maintenance contracts.

75.   Schools should keep a standard log book for recording events. Retained in a secure place, on site, available to the keyholder, it can contain useful information that will greatly assist both experienced and new keyholders. Typically, premises address, emergency telephone numbers and installation equipment details are included as a preface to the log book. Maintenance activity and alarm events are logged against the relevant circuit, area of protection, and specific detector details. Recording methods may be easily tailored to suit the requirements of the particular LEA.

6 Operation of intruder alarm systems

76. Human factors have a great impact upon the satisfactory operation of intruder alarms. Lack of discipline will cause security exposures resulting from alarm systems not being properly armed and the occurrences of excessive false alarms leading to the withdrawal of police response. Approximately 95% of intruder alarm activations are attributed to false alarms. Technical advances in hand with good design and installation practice will drastically reduce the occurrence of equipment induced false alarms. However it is up to the user to employ operating methods that complement the high levels of technical standard that can now be achieved.

Setting of alarm system controls

77. Users of intruder alarm systems are generally non-technical people. To carry out the control panel setting procedure and subsequently reach and secure the final exit door, within a defined time, can be a daunting task for many people. The temptation may be to take a chance and not activate the alarm system, particularly where during previous setting procedures, accidental false alarms have already occurred. Inevitably, this lax situation continues until a loss investigation reveals that the alarm system has not been properly used.

78. User education is vital. LEAs should ensure that their tenders for alarm installations include a provision for adequate user training. Only by fulfilling this criterion will the user have the confidence to master the operational procedures. Frequently there will be a group of people with responsibility for operating the alarm system at different scheduled times. A formal management process should ensure that knowledge is shared within the operating group *guaranteeing* that new or relief staff are fully familiar with the alarm system controls.

79. LEAs can benefit by standardising upon a short list of suitable proprietary control panels. This ensures that relief and other staff transferred to unfamiliar premises are already familiar with the standards of controls. Further to this the LEAs in-house engineer or security specialist may beneficially be charged with the responsibility to support the user educational needs. This has particular bearing where an intruder alarm installation is either new or has undergone significant modifications.

User induced false alarms

80. False alarms induced by the user are avoidable and should therefore be eliminated by the adoption of good management procedures. The operator of an intruder alarm system should follow a defined routine prior to activating or de-activating the alarm system. Before attempting to set the system all protected doors and windows should be physically secured. A visual inspection of protected areas should confirm that heaters and fans are switched off together with other false alarm-inducing environmental factors. Similarly the inspection should check that boxes and other materials are not stored in an insecure manner whereby they may be liable to move under the influences of a draught or vibration. The final exit route should be clear and free of stored materials, wedged doors or other factors that may impede movement through the exit route. The operator of the alarm system should be fully prepared before attempting the entry procedure. Prior to opening the first entry door the operator should ensure that all other relevant keys are readily available to gain access to the controls and disarm the control panel. In respect of this the operator will need to have available keys to any intermediate doors together with the operating key for the control panel or be prepared to enter the appropriate code upon a control panel digital keypad.

81. Sensible methods of key management greatly reduce the level of user induced false alarms. Often, a legitimate member of staff may possess a side door or other secondary key and use it to make entry to the school during unoccupied periods. Teachers are known to visit schools during holiday periods, perhaps to tend animals and plants, or to monitor long-term laboratory experiments. LEAs should ensure that out of business hours access is by prior arrangement with the building keeper or other person responsible for operating the alarm system. As a basic matter of security, keys should only be available to those members of staff with an essential need. In respect of this authorised keyholders should not casually delegate responsibility for opening or securing the premises.

82. For many premises zero false alarms can be a reality. Essentially intruder alarm installations should be of high standard and school staff must be made aware of the importance of enforcing the effective management of intruder alarm systems together with the whole concept of building security.

7 Case studies

The four studies represent typical examples of good practice that can be found in different types of schools. Taken from various parts of England they demonstrate cost effective intruder alarm installations that have been designed to balance the amount of protection provided to suit the amount of risk involved. This method achieves the optimum amount of protection where only limited finance is available to provide protection in a number of high risk schools.

SCHEDULE OF SYMBOLS

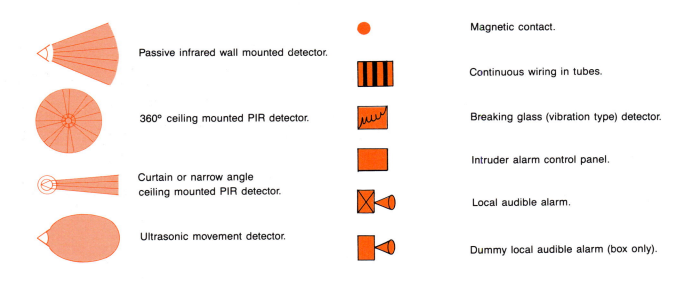

Passive infrared wall mounted detector.

360° ceiling mounted PIR detector.

Curtain or narrow angle ceiling mounted PIR detector.

Ultrasonic movement detector.

Magnetic contact.

Continuous wiring in tubes.

Breaking glass (vibration type) detector.

Intruder alarm control panel.

Local audible alarm.

Dummy local audible alarm (box only).

Symbols have been devised for the purpose of this publication. BS 4737 is currently being revised to include a section on symbols.

A large middle school in the Midlands

83.   The school was constructed during the 1980s and derives most of its intake from a nearby large council estate. The site is also occupied by a sports centre and two other schools, all of which had previously been provided with alarm systems.

84.   The rear elevations of this school face an expanse of open fields at the boundary of which is a choice of getaway routes for the intruder. Historically the school has suffered from a very high rate of break-ins resulting in theft and vandalism. This was considered to be partly due to the geographical vulnerability of the school and the fact that the older buildings on the same site were already protected with intruder alarm systems.

85.   In the 12 months since the installation of the intruder alarm system there has been a drastic decrease in the number of break-ins. When break-ins do occur the alarm system has always activated and caused the intruders to make an empty-handed retreat. Unfortunately, the elevated position of the

school offers the intruder a vantage point from which the intruder may observe the police approaching at considerable distance and therefore have ample time to effect their escape. However the sounding of the local audible alarm and the approaching police car means that the attempted theft is abandoned.

86.   Protection has been provided to circulation and target areas at ground floor level with a small number of detectors situated on the first floor where adjacent flat roofs enable easy access to break in at first floor level. The illustrated plan has been marked up to indicate the location of particular intruder alarm components including the use of the recently-introduced ceiling-mounted type of detector where there is often an advantage in reduced levels of physical damage. In general, the philosophy of this particular example has also been applied in the other examples of good practice detailed herein. In 1986 the alarm system cost approximately £1,900 to install.

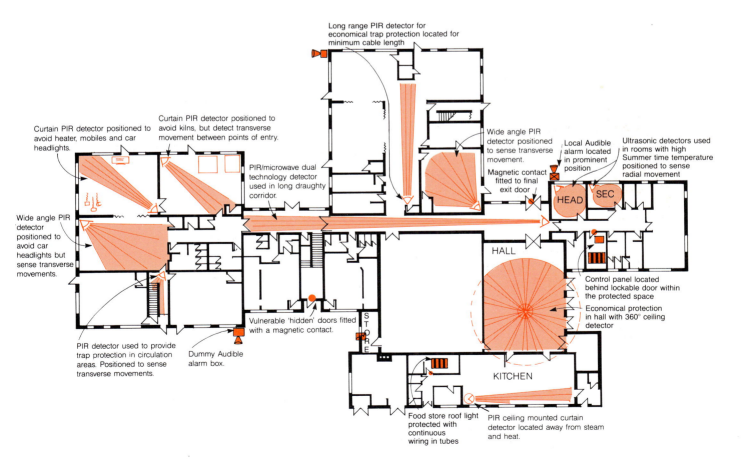

A small Victorian first and middle school in London

87. The school fronts onto a well-lit residential road but its side and rear elevations face an open industrial site, a secluded public footpath and an access route to the rear of commercial premises and are therefore generally hidden from public view. This school was persistently troubled by break-ins where the intruders were intent upon theft, vandalism or arson. The alarm system was installed in 1985 and in the following two years there was only one incident of a break-in which resulted in damage to windows and the school piano which was located in the hall. Subsequently, this particular intruder was later arrested during a break-in at another school when the intruder alarm system alerted police. This basic alarm system, with scope for future extension, was installed for less than £500. Illustrated is the very effective use of just three detectors where one corridor detector at ground floor level not only provides trap protection to the ground floor but serves to detect intruders attempting to gain access to the first floor offices. Finance has recently become available to economically extend the system to protect the side and rear elevations.

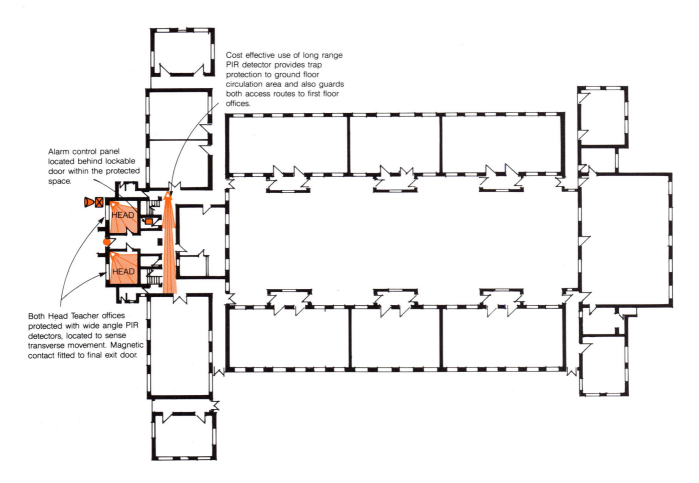

Cost effective use of long range PIR detector provides trap protection to ground floor circulation area and also guards both access routes to first floor offices.

Alarm control panel located behind lockable door within the protected space.

Both Head Teacher offices protected with wide angle PIR detectors, located to sense transverse movement. Magnetic contact fitted to final exit door.

A large comprehensive school incorporating a continuing education centre in Southern England

88. The ground floor plan only of this three-storey 1950s building is illustrated. In more recent years, additional buildings have been added to cater for the local rise in pupil numbers. The school contains a great deal of valuable items and is particularly vulnerable to intruders since three of its elevations are hidden from public view and back on to fields through which there is a network of public footpaths. Within the constraints of limited finance, the school was considered too large to provide comprehensive protection. With this in mind it was decided to install trap protection in circulation areas with point protection in high risk target areas. Historically, there had been a number of break-ins at first floor level where adjacent single-storey flat roof buildings had been used to gain access. A small number of detectors have therefore been installed to provide trap protection at first floor level where it meets adjacent flat roofed areas. The school suffers from noise and vibrations caused by low-flying aircraft and for this reason the use of microwave or ultrasonic detection devices was not considered. The system has been highly effective as a deterrent having significantly reduced the level of break-ins. Arrests have resulted from the police responding to the alarm system's signal. In 1985 the system cost less than £1,600 and has proved itself effective and reliable. However the low cost control panel is not convenient to flexible zoning or changes in patterns of occupancy.

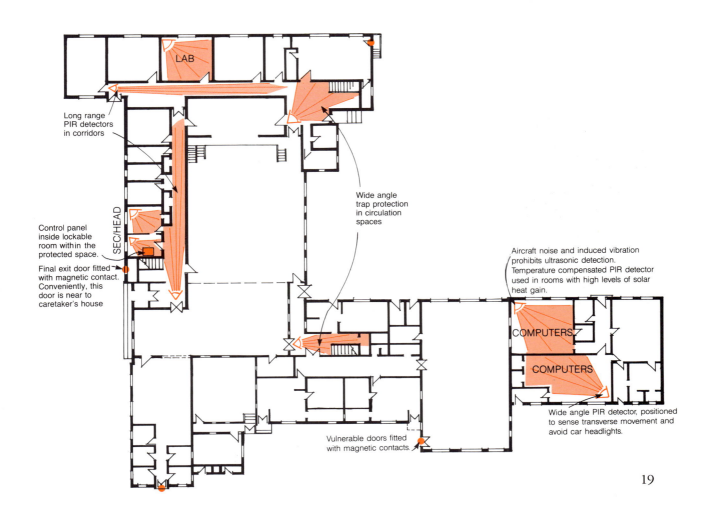

Long range PIR detectors in corridors

Control panel inside lockable room within the protected space.

Final exit door fitted with magnetic contact. Conveniently, this door is near to caretaker's house

SEC/HEAD

LAB

Wide angle trap protection in circulation spaces

Aircraft noise and induced vibration prohibits ultrasonic detection. Temperature compensated PIR detector used in rooms with high levels of solar heat gain.

COMPUTERS

COMPUTERS

Wide angle PIR detector, positioned to sense transverse movement and avoid car headlights.

Vulnerable doors fitted with magnetic contacts.

CDT Centre at a North of England school

89. It was decided to dedicate one of the two 1930s built school buildings to form a CDT centre. Due to the very high risks associated with valuable equipment it was considered worthwhile to install a high degree of protection against intruders. Occupancy periods are considerably extended due to community participation in CDT subjects. A separate intruder alarm system has been installed in each school building in order to ease the problems associated with managing the security of two buildings with greatly differing occupancy patterns. The schools are provided with multiplex control panels which have been found useful in catering for the flexible zoning requirements to suit the changing patterns of use. During the two years that the system has been in use there have been no false alarms either induced by the users or technical failure.

90. Good forward planning ensured that the alarm system was installed at the same time that expensive CDT equipment was installed. Recognising the extent of the risk it was decided to provide intruder alarm protection from the onset. There have been a small number of break-ins but they have always been abandoned upon the activation of the alarm system with the losses being restricted to minor damage only. In 1986 the system cost approximately £1,400.

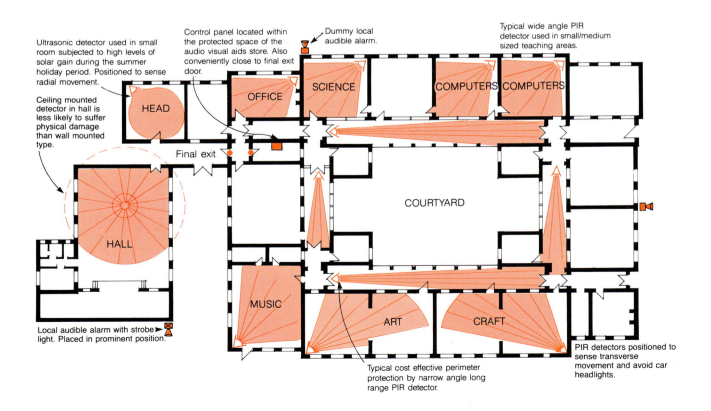

Ultrasonic detector used in small room subjected to high levels of solar gain during the summer holiday period. Positioned to sense radial movement.

Control panel located within the protected space of the audio visual aids store. Also conveniently close to final exit door.

Dummy local audible alarm.

Typical wide angle PIR detector used in small/medium sized teaching areas.

Ceiling mounted detector in hall is less likely to suffer physical damage than wall mounted type.

HEAD

OFFICE

SCIENCE

COMPUTERS COMPUTERS

Final exit

COURTYARD

HALL

Local audible alarm with strobe light. Placed in prominent position.

MUSIC

ART

CRAFT

Typical cost effective perimeter protection by narrow angle long range PIR detector.

PIR detectors positioned to sense transverse movement and avoid car headlights.

APPENDICES

APPENDIX 1   Intruder detection devices

91.   The devices used to detect the presence of an intruder are usually either electronic sensors of movement or electrical components that are positioned to detect physical actions such as foot pressure, doors opening, or glass breaking. Since the introduction of the microprocessor to security applications, movement detectors have become the most common forms of intruder detection. Table 2 indicates the main factors that influence the range of detection and the false alarm risk.

92.   This appendix describes many of the forms of detection starting with the three main types of electronic movement detectors.

ULTRASONIC 'VOLUMETRIC' DETECTORS

Theory of operation

93.   Ultrasonic detectors use high frequency sound waves to sense the presence of an intruder in a protected space.

94.   Early generations of ultrasonic detectors were inherently unstable because they were adversely affected by ambient environmental factors. However, present day ultrasonic devices, incorporating microprocessors, are much more reliable and should be evaluated according to their specification and be objectively compared with other devices in terms of levels of security and the environmental conditions that relate to any particular situation. Correctly used, reliable, higher levels of security can be achieved with the ultrasonic detector.

95.   Ultrasonic 'volumetric' movement detectors perform three main functions:

■   Transmission of ultrasonic sound waves into the protected space.

■   Reception of ultrasonic sound waves reflected back from "mass" within the protected space.

■   Electronic processing of the received ultrasonic sound waves, using the transmitted signal as a reference of comparison. The various stages of processing analyse changes imposed upon the received signal. Changes have different

characteristics depending upon the factor which acted upon the reflected wave. Within limitations, a human body can be electronically differentiated from an enviromental disturbance such as air turbulence above a room heater. The quality of this electronic filtering is the prime factor in establishing immunity to false alarms and may eliminate the problem associated with earlier ultrasonic detectors.

96.   Present day ultrasonic detectors are available with two separate alarm outputs: No. 1 to signal a full alarm condition; No. 2 is normally an "electronic switch" which enables a small current to pass through a transistor within the detector to signify an alert (near alarm) condition. When used in conjunction with an "intelligent" or similarly compatible control panel this electronic output can be used to give advanced warning of environmental factors that "almost" activated an alarm condition. Additionally some detectors incorporate further circuitry that monitors the functioning of the detector's components and creates an alert via the electronic output when a detector's performance deviates beyond a pre-set tolerance. This also protects against accidental or deliberate masking (see glossary) of the detector. In high security areas, with a stable environment the electronic output No. 2 may be used together with output No. 1 to provide a very sensitive detector that will activate an alarm under either output mode. For high security application, detectors are available that can be tested remotely, whilst they remain actively in use. However it is essential to ensure that detectors and control panels are compatible for the options required.

97.   Since the sensitivity (range) of an ultrasonic detector varies with ambient temperature, some detectors incorporate auto-compensators that automatically compensate for temperature variations.

98.   Generally ultrasonic detectors are not effective in rooms larger than $10m^2$ or smaller than about $3m^2$. Where multiple detectors are used in a single area, directions of coverage should be parallel.

Requirements for ultrasonic detectors

99.   Ultrasonic detectors should generally meet the following requirements:

TABLE 2

EFFECTS OF ENVIRONMENTAL FACTORS ON RANGE OF DETECTION AND FALSE ALARM RISK			
FACTOR	PIR	U/S	M/W
Level of ambient temperature nears body temperature.	●		
Rapid temperature change.	●	○	
Level of humidity.	○	○	
Air movement.	○	◐	
Weather conditions: thunder, lightning, hail.	○	◐	◐
Sunlight cast into detector.	◐		
Vibration.	○	●	●
Loud noise.		◐	○
Heaters within field of coverage.	◐	○	
Soft furnishings and curtains.	○	◐	○
Vehicle lights or other moving lights cast into detector.	◐		
Moving/falling objects: mobiles, Christmas decorations, curtains, posters, signs etc.	◐	◐	◐
Detection of movement behind glass and lightweight structures.			●
Movement of small animals and close range insects.	◐	◐	◐
Fluid flowing in non metallic pipes.			●
Stray detection of movement due to reflections off metal surfaces.			◐
Use of air lines or other release of pressurised gases.		◐	

FALSE ALARM RISK	
Slight	○
Moderate	◐
Severe	●

PIR = Passive infrared.
U/S = Ultrasonic.
M/W = Microwave.

EFFECT ON RANGE	
Slight	○
Moderate	◐
Severe	●

- Operate at a frequency above 22 kHz, typically 25-35 kHz. Crystal controlled, piezo ceramic-transducers enable detectors to operate in the same area without suffering from cross interference.

- Operate on the Doppler Effect (see glossary) employing processing circuitry to detect frequency shift between transmitted signal and received signal, as may be caused by a moving human target.

- Employ high quality active filtering to fully and effectively discriminate between Doppler Effects due to "human intruder" and background environmental disturbance. The amplitude time basis principle is inadequate for high levels of discrimination and accordingly it should not be used.

- Be fitted with a range adjuster.

- Provide temperature compensation for applications below 12°C and above 30°C.

- Be capable of satisfactory operation under the following environmental conditions:
  Temperature: − 10°C to + 50°C
  Relative humidity: 0% - 90%
  N.B. Very low and very high levels of humidity extend the range of detection and may expose a false alarm risk

- Suitability for their application, either wall, or corner mounted. Some detectors are universal. Special detectors with a splayed transmitter receiver arrangements are necessary for ceiling mounted applications, in order to sense predominantly transverse movement.

- Incorporate a tamper circuit to activate an alarm condition when the cover has been removed or the unit has been physically damaged.

- Provide light emitting diodes (LEDs) for walk testing and optionally latch-on after an alarm condition (but not prior to initiation of the entry procedure) until reset, thus indicating the point of intrusion or faulty detector identification. It is desirable that detectors enable the walk test mode to be remotely extinguished during normal occupancy, and only respond when the control panel is set in the test mode. Detectors and control panels must be chosen for their compatibility to match the options required.

- Self monitoring circuitry with reporting of detector or environmental abnormalities may be used to advantage in conjunction with "intelligent" or other compatible control panels. Remote testing compatibility is useful.

- To be secured to the base with a screw, and not rely solely on plastic lug retainers.

Environmental factors

100. Detector and environmental compatibility is essential to achieve high levels of security with zero false alarms. Although good quality detectors with circuit processing incorporating active filters inherently have some immunity to environmental factors, this must not be taken as a reason to permit ultrasonic detectors to be misused and placed in unsuitable environments. This approach would lead to generally reduced levels of security and certainly increase the incidence of false alarms. The following list itemises environmental factors that could adversely affect the operation of an ultrasonic detector:

- Minimum sensitivity (range) for a detector in its basic form would occur at about 30°C. Either side of this temperature the range increases. At 5°C the range might be 30% greater and similarly at 50°C the range may be increased by 10%, therefore some ultrasonic detectors' range and performance can change with environmental variations. BS 4737: part 3 requires detectors to operate satisfactorily in 0°C to 40°C bands. Detectors with temperature compensation reduce the amount of range variance with temperature.

- The amounts of moisture in the air in the space protected has a direct bearing upon the range of detection. At exceptionally high or low levels of relative humidity the ultrasonic detector's range becomes most extended. Minimum sensitivity occurs at about 30% relative humidity.

- Turbulence and draughts can induce a Doppler Effect upon the transmitted ultrasonic wave form causing false alarms. Modern detectors have a reasonable degree of immunity to such turbulence but this is unlikely to deal effectively with air movement produced by mechanical ventilation, or fan assisted heaters.

- The surface to which the detector is fixed must be free from vibration. Do not mount detectors to a surface that may have vibrations imposed upon it, whilst the alarm is active. In light-weight buildings partition walls may vibrate during storm conditions. It is essential that objects within the range of detection do not produce vibrations within the periods when the alarm is active.

- Many mechanical and electrical pieces of apparatus produce ultrasonic sound and these may result in false alarms. The designer should be aware of the possibility of ultrasonic sound infiltration from external sources. Even air blowing through a keyhole may produce a whistle with a harmonic ultrasonic wave form. Recently introduced electronic ballasts for

Fig. 2   Ultrasonic volumetric movement detectors

Side views of typical coverage patterns

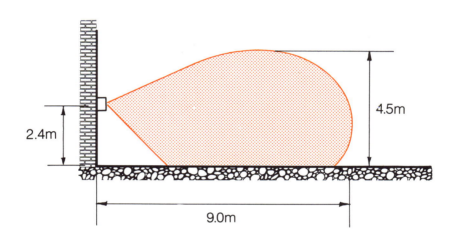

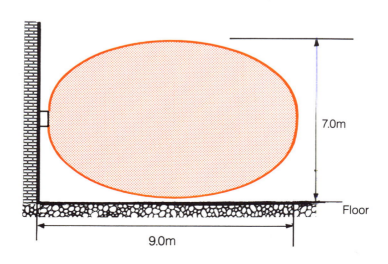

Plan views of typical coverage patterns.

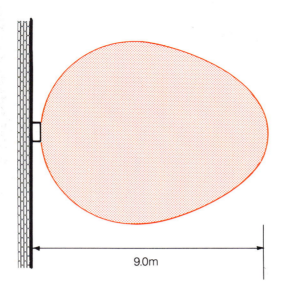

9.0m

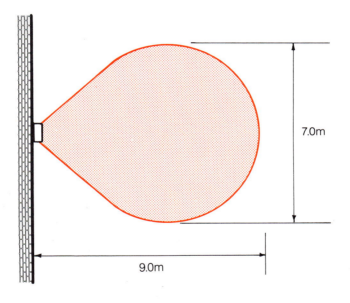

7.0m

9.0m

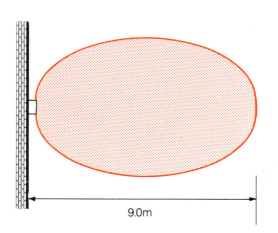

9.0m

(Figure 2 continued)

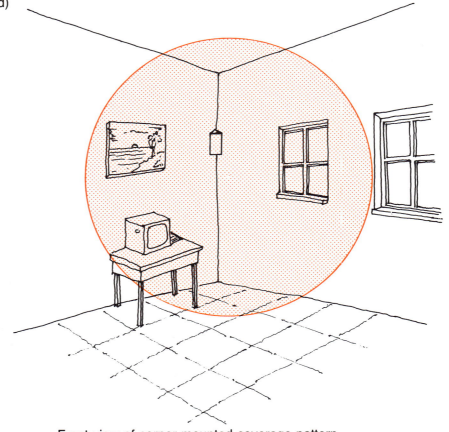

Front view of corner mounted coverage pattern.

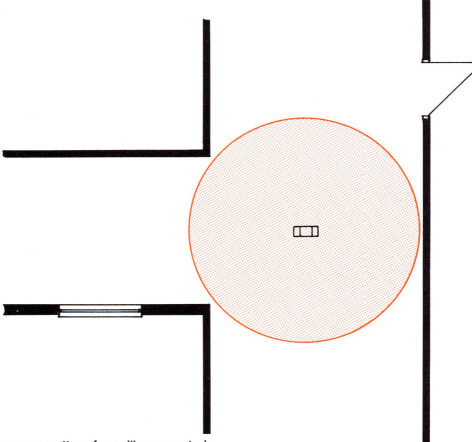

Plan view of coverage pattern for ceiling mounted detector. Ceiling must not be subjected to vibration.

fluorescent lighting operate at about 28 kHz and may produce ultrasonic sound waves causing a false alarm.

■ The material composition and location of solid objects within the protected space will affect the performance of ultrasonic detectors. Soft furnishings absorb ultrasonic waves whilst hard surfaces act as reflectors. Following rearrangements it is essential that a "walk test" is carried out to ensure adequate sensitivity and the absence of masking of the detector. Any solid object which is likely to move may well cause a false alarm, although some detectors may filter out typical patterns of disturbance cause by such incidences as a small sign slightly swaying in a draught. Ultrasonic detectors do not penetrate glass, timber or masonry.

■ Normal statutorily controlled broadcasting systems are very unlikely to cause an ultrasonic detector to activate an alarm. Exceptionally, unauthorised transmitting or faulty transmitters may radiate low frequency radio waves creating a false alarm hazard. Ultrasonic detectors, sited close to poorly suppressed electrical or electronic equipment, may also carry a similar risk. Unfortunately radio frequency interference is difficult to foresee but should be considered when investigating successive false alarms.

Commissioning notes

101. The installer should aim to adjust the sensitivity control to suit conditions applicable to the periods of unoccupancy when the alarm system will be active. In conjunction with this, environmental factors, temperature, humidity and air movement are most relevant. Where these conditions cannot be simulated the engineer should use his best judgement to compensate the setting of the sensitivity adjuster. Proprietary testers are available to check for the presence of unwanted ultrasonic sound.

102. Under conditions of motionless air and also low humidity, which may occur most frequently during periods of unoccupancy, the range of the ultrasonic detector may become extended thus creating the risk of alarms being activated by motion occurring at a greater distance than appreciated during walk testing at commissioning. Ultrasonic detectors are most sensitive to radial (towards or away) movement, and should be positioned with this in mind.

103. Refer to commissioning detailed in section 4.

104. Figure 2 illustrates typical patterns of coverage but the shape of the space under protection

may sometimes slightly widen or elongate the actual pattern of coverage.

MICROWAVE 'VOLUMETRIC' DETECTORS

Theory of operation

105. Microwave detectors, as the name implies, use low power microwaves to detect the presence of an intruder. The basic principle of operation may be compared with that of the ultrasonic detector. The main difference being that ultrasonic detectors rely upon air as the medium to carry the ultrasonic sound wave, whereas the propagation of the electromagnetic wave produced by the microwave detector is independent of air. Consequently, the environmental factors such as air turbulence, temperature and humidity do not directly affect the microwave detector. Unfortunately, since the microwave is inherently a radio signal, there are certain adverse aspects associated with the microwave movement detector.

106. The relatively high rate of false alarms attributed to the microwave detector is generally due to the device responding to events outside the desired field of coverage. The detector is not unreliable in itself but its poor reputation stems from it being sited in unsuitable locations or incorrectly set in a too sensitive operating mode. However, modern detectors, incorporating microprocessor technology have a reasonable degree of immunity to false alarms and may well have a useful role in those applications not suited to passive infrared or ultrasonic devices. The designer should not therefore disregard the existence of the microwave detector.

107. Indeed, in certain environmental conditions, they may be the only workable form of movement detection. Most types of detector need to be specified to be compatible with their operating environment, and none more so than the microwave device.

108. Whilst there is no evidence that exposure to very low levels of microwave energy constitutes a health risk, it may be prudent to avoid siting detectors close to persons in spaces of sustained occupancy. Alternatively some control systems can switch off detectors during the occupancy periods.

109. Microwave 'volumetric' movement detectors perform three main functions.

■ Transmit a beamed microwave signal into the space under protection.

- Receive microwave signals reflected back from 'mass' within the protected space.

- Electronically process the received microwave signal using the transmitted signal as a reference. This method relies upon Doppler Effect which occurs when some of the received signal has been reflected off a moving object.

110. Modern microwave detectors incorporating processing circuitry, usually in the form of integrated circuits, hold considerable advantages over their less technically sophisticated predecessors that were condemned as a source of false alarms. However, microwave devices have less tolerance to misuse and adverse environments, accordingly expert knowledge is needed to select the right detector for the right job. These notes are intended to assist, but they should be read in conjunction with the technical specification of any proposed microwave detector.

Requirements for microwave detectors

111. Microwave detectors should meet the following requirements:

- Operate in the microwave frequency band width at a particular frequency which satisfies local regulations. For the United Kingdom this frequency is currently 10.687 kHz.

- The transmitted pattern of coverage as detailed in the manufacturer's polar plot, to be compatible with the dimensions of the volume of space under protection. Normally, options exist regarding length of range and shape of beam. For long range detectors, the microwave energy is generally "focused" in a thin pencil-like beam, whilst short and medium range are available with a wide angle projected beam, of 15 metres to 30 metres range.

- Operate under the Doppler Effect, employing processing circuitry to detect frequency differences between the transmitted signal and the received signal and employ further stages of processing circuitry to discriminate between Doppler Effect due to a "human intruder" and that caused by random factors such as small objects swaying in a draught.

- Incorporate a high degree of immunity to radio frequency interference. Physical screening may be provided by the detector's casing.

- Include a supply voltage regulator, with filtering against transient and other line interference.

- Be fitted with an easy-to-use range adjustment. A separate sensitivity control is advantageous.

- Include tamper connections to signal a warning when the detector cover is removed or when the detector has become physically damaged. The cover to be screw fixed.

- Be protected against the ingress of dust, small insects and moisture

- Be normally capable of operating in a temperature range of: −10°C to +50°C.

- For installation where more than one microwave detector is likely to be used, detectors should include mutual interference immunity circuits. Ensure that fields of coverage do not overlap. In particular direction of coverage should be parallel.

- LED walk test indicator light to be fitted with a facility to provide an option for it to be remotely extinguished during periods of building occupancy. Note: this prevents building occupants testing the range of detection.

- Incorporate a "latch on" facility for the LED. In conjunction with a compatible control panel the LED will indicate the detector that initiated an alarm or responded to a fault condition.

- Incorporate a facility for the alarm relay to be remotely disabled whilst the control panel is in the occupancy mode. This significantly reduces wear to the alarm relay. A similar facility to switch off the microwave transmitter is advantageous, particularly when it is desired, for any reason, to prevent occupants being subjected to low levels of microwave energy radiation.

- Include self monitoring circuitry to warn of pending detector fault, or masking of detector. Also to advise "near alarm" occurrence. These features should be signalled by a separate output and can be used to advantage with "intelligent" and other compatible control panels. In conjunction with this output the detector LED should illuminate when the control panel is in the test or the normal daytime occupancy mode. Exact arrangement will depend upon the specification of the control panel used in this application.

- Incorporate the facility to enable remote testing from the control panel or a distant central station.

Environmental factors

112. For microwave detectors, environmental compatibility is extremely important. Although microwave detectors possess some false alarm immunity to factors such as air turbulence, and

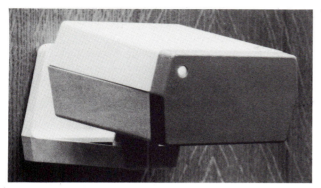

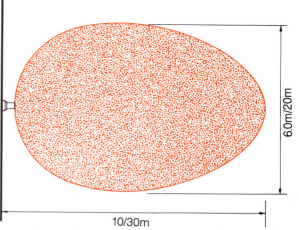

Fig. 3 Typical microwave volumetric coverage pattern in free space. Separate units are made with ranges between 10m and 30m.

6.0m/20m

10/30m

other climatic changes they are, unfortunately, sensitive to less obvious environmental factors, such as movement behind walls, and radio frequency interference.

113.   The following list highlights typical environmental factors which may adversely affect the operation of microwave detectors:

- Microwave detectors can "see" through glass, timber, lightweight building blocks and plaster. Hence "out of sight" movement behind seemingly solid screens may activate a false alarm. (Adjust range to fall short of walls where false alarm risks exist.) Even air ducts may carry detection into adjacent areas. (Avoid directing detector at external walls, doors and windows.)

- Mirrors and all metallic surfaces will reflect microwaves and may create unexpected new areas of detection, leading to false alarms. (Avoid directing beams at filing cabinets and other metallic objects.) Metallic objects also create a shadow in the field of coverage where intruders may pass undetected.

- The detector should be suited to its mounting position, either wall, ceiling or corner fixed. The detector must be positioned to detect movement, by the intruder, that is predominantly towards or away from the detector. Microwave detectors have far less response to movement across the field of coverage, this is due to the reduced Doppler Effect created by transverse motion.

- Microwave detectors may be hidden behind lightweight building materials. Where occupancy vandalism is a consideration, detectors may be employed to 'look through' ceilings and partition walls. In that application it is essential to ensure that plasterboard is not backed by aluminium foil.

- Small animals, even fish in an aquarium, may activate a false alarm.

- Vibration is a major source of false alarms. (Fix detector to a solid structure.) Partition walls

and some ceilings may vibrate from the effects of traffic, aircraft or thunder.

- Avoid installing microwave detectors directly underneath flight paths where high levels of aviation noise may exist. Circumstances may also arise whereby aircraft navigation aids activate microwave devices.

- Set range and adjust detector such that it will not "look through" materials and activate false alarms due to: heavy rain, hail; or birds on a roof. Also water passing through non-metallic pipes may activate a false alarm.

- Do not permit objects subjected to draught movement to fall within the detector's range. The slightest movement of an aluminium venetian blind will activate a false alarm. Suspended signs constitute a similar risk.

- When in use fluorescent and other electrical discharge lights may activate a false alarm.

- The range of detection may be modified according to the use of the space under protection. Furniture and other physical objects introduced to the protected space will create the need for walk testing to be repeated. Accordingly, readjustment to range or siting of the detector may be necessary.

- Electrical equipment, particularly rotating machinery, and also certain mobile radio transmissions, may activate false alarms.

Commissioning notes

114.   The importance of walk testing cannot be overstated. Ensure that movement within the whole of the space intended to be protected will activate an alarm condition. Also walk test behind closed doors and walls to verify that the detector will not

activate an alarm from motion within a legitimately occupied area. Similarly, as far as is practicable, check for false alarms arising from environmental factors such as passing vehicles, fluorescent lighting, and water flowing in pipes.

115. Proprietary testers are a useful aid to setting range and identifying the presence of radio frequency interference. In respect of this ensure that the signal to noise ratio is compatible to the detector's specification and operating parameters.

116. Adjust the range control to the absolute minimum setting that is necessary to extend the field of coverage adequately into the desired area of protection.

117. Refer to commissioning as detailed within section 4.

118. Figure 3 illustrates the typical free space pattern of coverage of the microwave detector. Physical objects may distort patterns of coverage.

PASSIVE INFRARED DETECTORS

Theory of operation

119. Passive infrared (PIR) detectors work by sensing an intruder's body heat. In this sense PIR detectors are not movement detectors. They are sensors of infrared radiation. However, specially designed optics and circuit processing enable the device to respond to movement by reacting to changes in infrared radiation, brought about by movement of the intruder within the volume of space under protection.

120. PIR detectors have 5 main parts.

Sensors (detectors of infrared energy)

121. These are pyroelectric devices, which absorb heat from the infrared rays directed on them. This produces a voltage output that is subsequently used to operate the alarm relay.

122. Recently, dual element infrared detectors have been produced. These comprise a single enclosure, about the size of an aspirin, housing two separate sensor elements. Looking to the future it seems probable that multi-element sensors units will succeed the two-element unit. With detectors containing two or more sensors, greater false alarm immunity can be achieved. 'Quad' detectors normally employ two dual element sensors, to provide four element sections.

Optical filters

123. The infrared energy emitted by the human body and objects at room temperature fall within the spectrum range of 7-14 micro metres wavelength. Accordingly filters are selected to transmit this particular spectrum only and thus form a barrier to other infrared energy frequencies produced by environmental factors and thereby eliminating certain false alarm hazards. In the earlier passive infrared detectors the filter formed a separate component but this is now generally to be found as a component part of the hermetically sealed sensor device.

Optical (lens and mirrors)

124. The optics of a detector determines the field of coverage and the number of sensitive zones. Essentially, the optics direct the infrared energy from the field of coverage onto the heads of the sensor elements. The quality of the optics has a direct bearing on the signal to noise ratio of the electronic signal output and is particularly important in the case of long-range applications. Main types of optics are parabolic mirrors and Fresnel lens for single zone detectors and multi-parabolic mirrors and complex Fresnel lens for multi-zone applications. Generally the Fresnel lens is a composite part of the front cover making it vulnerable to deliberate damage. Dust may also accumulate on the lens. Detectors employing the Fresnel lens are best used in applications serving small areas where the risk of physical damage is negligible.

125. Lenses employing highly reflective mirrors provide a precision optical field of coverage and are highly efficient at directing the infrared energy on to a sensor head. A further optical refinement compensates for size and distance of the target, thereby reducing false alarm risks from insects and rodents at close range whilst at the same time giving good sensitivity at the periphery of the field of coverage to human size targets. In effect, a target of a given size will cause the same infrared change imposed upon the sensor head whether the target is in the near or distant area of the field of coverage.

Case and Lens Cover

126. Many passive infrared detectors have flimsy covers which have little resistance to damage induced by the opportunist vandal who may only need apply finger pressure to sustain damage. However considerably more durable materials are available and quality detectors can be obtained with improved resistance to wanton damage. Dome-shaped ceiling-mounted detectors offer improved

resistance to physical damage. Covers should be securely fixed to their base and not rely upon plastic clips.

Electronic circuitry

127. There are more manufacturers of passive infrared detectors than any other form of movement sensor. Advances in electronic circuit technology and competition between manufacturers has led to different patented techniques being used to produce highly sensitive detectors with enhanced immunity to false alarms.

128. For difficult environments sensors with "quad" or double dual element methods have special advantages. In this type of detector any change in infrared radiation that simultaneously falls upon all sensor elements will normally be disregarded as of environmental origin and prevented from causing a false alarm. Only when the sequence and amplitude of received infrared radiation imposed upon the elements is typical of that induced by intruder motion, will an alarm be activated by the circuitry. Further false alarm immunity can be achieved by circuitry which is designed to sense two or maybe three intruder motion signals within a defined period, say 20 seconds. Only when this condition has been satisfied will an alarm signal be activated. With such a large variety of PIR detectors on the market it should be possible to select a detector to suit any given situation.

Requirements for passive infrared detectors

129. PIR detectors should generally meet the following requirements:

The detector should comply with BS 4737: Part 3, Section 3.7.

Operate by sensing a rapid change in levels of infrared energy emitted from the field of coverage.

Possess an optical lens of adequate quality with either highly reflective mirrors or where suitable, Fresnel lens.

The optical arrangement must produce the desired field of coverage.

Incorporate an optical filter to transmit only the 7-14 micro metre wavelengths.

Possess electronic circuit processing to discriminate between real and false alarm conditions. Sensitivity to real alarms not to be too compromised by false alarm immunity.

An LED to be provided to facilitate walk testing. Means to be provided to either extinguish or hide from view the LED to prevent building occupants gaining knowledge of field of coverage. Some detectors utilise an LED to indicate unacceptably high levels of background disturbance as an aid to commissioning.

A socket should, preferably, be provided on the detector to accept a plug from a hand-held tester. Such testers are available to assist in the commissioning and setting of sensitivity controls.

Detectors should not be used within areas less than 60% of their range if environmental false alarms are to be avoided.

Detectors with automatic temperature sensitivity adjustment can be used to advantage in environments of considerable temperature variation, particularly where high Summer temperatures occur. Generally, there must be a 2°C temperature difference between background and intruder body temperature for the device to operate reliably.

Detectors should be capable of satisfactory operation under the following environmental conditions:

Temperature: − 10°C to + 40°C.

Relative humidity: 10% to 90%

Self monitoring anti-blind PIR detectors, utilising their own infrared source to monitor, can considerably improve levels of security in high risk areas when used with compatible control panels. They are complementary to the other types of detector produced for use with 'intelligent' control panels.

Detectors should incorporate terminals for a tamper circuit. This should activate an alarm if the detector is physically damaged or if its cover is removed.

Where risks of physical damage exist, select detectors of a robust design. There is great variation in the physical strength of various detectors on the market. Covers secured by a locking screw are generally more effective than plastic clips. Ceiling mounted detectors are less likely to be vandalised or masked.

Traditional PIR detectors.

130. Designed for wall, corner or sometimes ceiling-mounted, the field of coverage varies from

Fig. 4   Wall mounted PIR detectors for general applications.

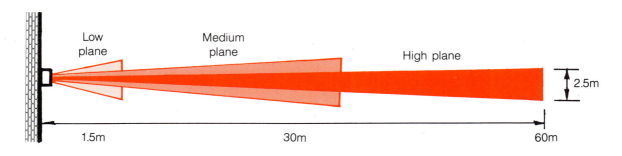

Typical plan of long range coverage pattern.

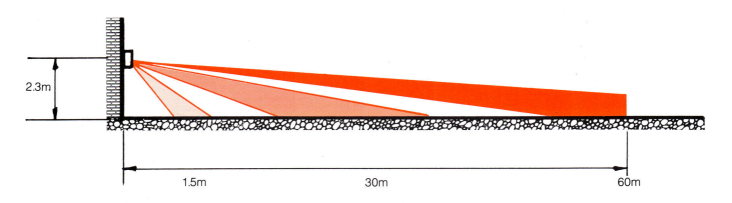

Typical side view of long range coverage pattern.

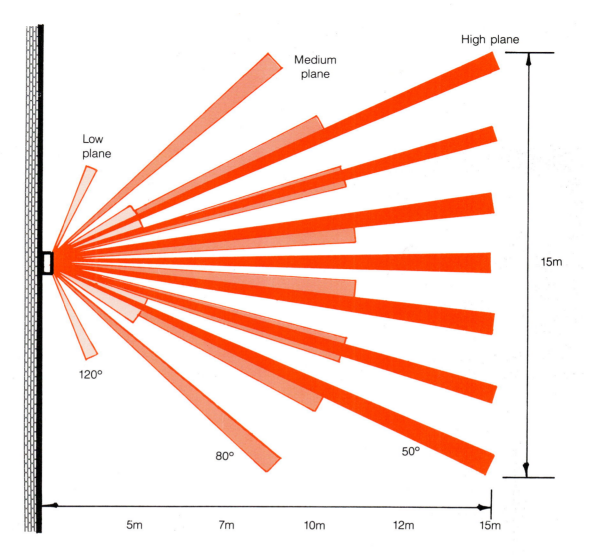

Typical plan view of wide angle coverage pattern.

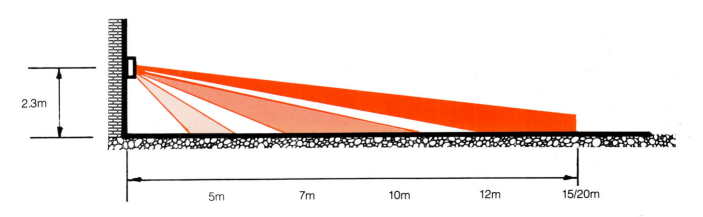

Typical side view of wide angle coverage pattern.

35

Fig. 5   Wall mounted PIR curtain detectors.

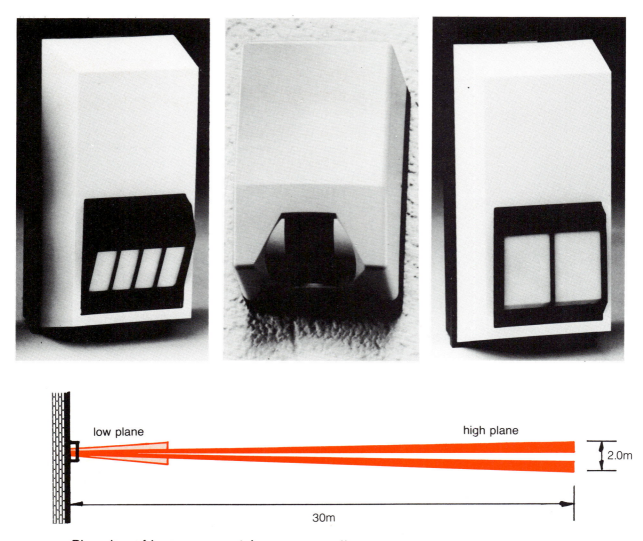

low plane   high plane

                                                                          2.0m

                          30m

Plan view of long range curtain coverage pattern.

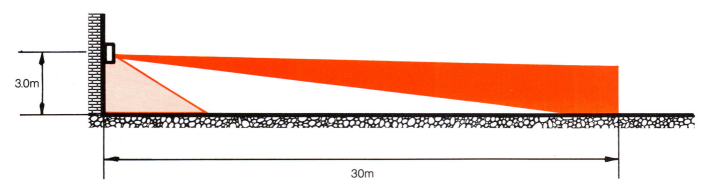

3.0m

                          30m

Side view of long range curtain coverage pattern

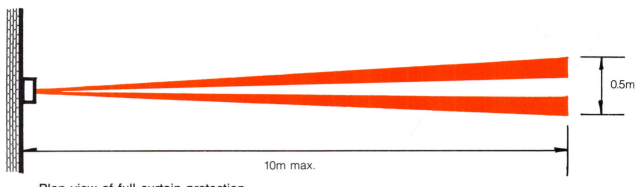

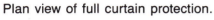

0.5m

10m max.

Plan view of full curtain protection.

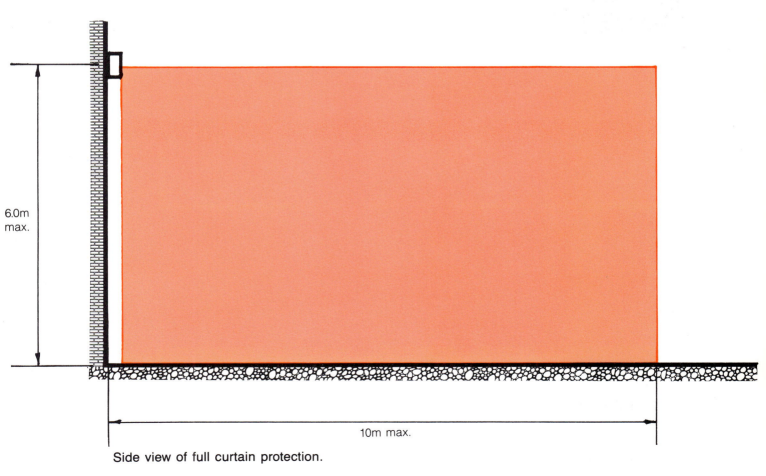

6.0m max.

10m max.

Side view of full curtain protection.

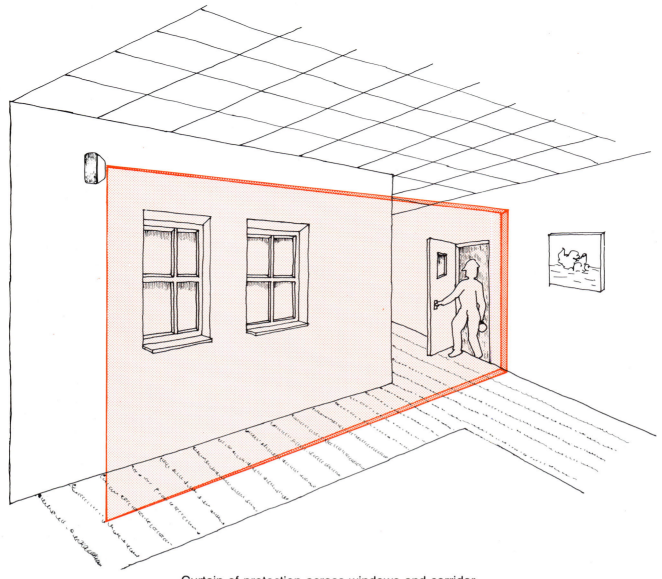

Curtain of protection across windows and corridor.
They are often used parallel to school computer room windows.

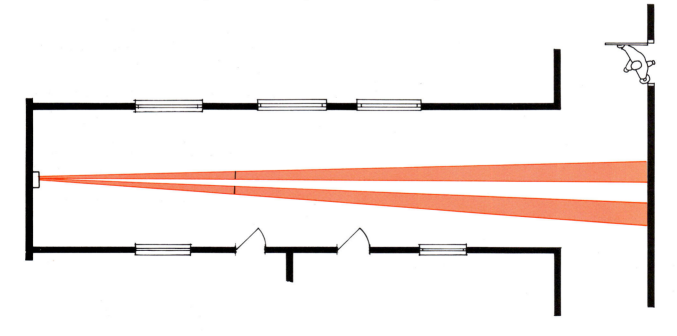

Long range curtain detector used in corridor application, positioned to detect transverse movement.

10m, wide angle, to 50m or greater, narrow angle long range detectors. The field of coverage is generally radial from the detector with sensitive zones emanating from the floor close to the detector and cast at intermediate coordinates rising to a zone cast at a height of about $2\frac{1}{2}$ m, towards the perimeter of the field of coverage. In general these detectors are intended to be wall-mounted at a height of 2.5 to 3.5m.

131. A variation of this type of detector comes in the form of a dome-shaped circular detector. It is intended for ceiling-mounting and the field of coverage may be variable and is therefore less obvious to the intruder, compared with the more traditional wall-mounted detector.

Curtain detectors

132. The optical arrangement of this type of detector produces a field of coverage that is unique to the PIR device. It cannot be emulated by the microwave or ultrasonic detector. The field of coverage produces the effect of an invisible wall of protection. The zones being cast directly above each other. The advantage of the curtain detector is its suitability to specific applications. The device may be used for example, to cast floor to ceiling protection immediately parallel to a large glazed area. Mounted at 90° the device may be used to cast a thin field of protection directly below a ceiling containing roof lights which could be a possible means of access to an intruder.

133. Since the invisible wall of protection can be aimed very selectively into the target area it is frequently possible to provide excellent levels of protection with unwanted environmental factors lying outside the field of view. False alarm risks are thus minimised. Generally, full curtain detectors have a maximum range of approximately 10m. Recently introduced long range models extend to about 45m but high level protection reduces towards the extremity of the range.

Ceiling-mounted detectors

134. Similar to PIR wall-mounted detectors, the ceiling mounted detector can be used in schools for wide angle, curtain or long range protection. Additionally, detectors are available that produce a complete 360° symmetrical field of coverage, making them ideally suited for use in assembly halls and other open areas where they may be positioned directly above target items. Although generally intended to be used with an all-round field of coverage of 360°, segments may be masked to screen specific environmental factors.

135. Being fabricated from relatively robust materials in the shape of a dome, they offer improved levels of vandal resistance. Similarly, ceiling mounting may often place them out of the vandal's reach. By means of a special bezel the units may be flush mounted into suspended ceilings, combining the benefits of a neat and discreet appearance with improved physical protection.

136. Ceiling-mounted detectors have a particular advantage in spaces liable to have furniture placed around the walls which may otherwise mask wall-mounted detectors. Also, being spherical in appearance it is difficult for the intruder to anticipate the field of coverage.

Environmental factors

137. Compared with microwave and ultrasonic devices PIR detectors have a greater basic immunity to most random environmental factors. The fundamental principle of operation of the PIR detector, in its basic form, is less sensitive to movement and random environmental factors than microwave or ultrasonic methods of detection. Noise and vibration cause very little problem. Also the range of coverage will not penetrate glass or other common building materials. The following environmental factors could effect the operation of PIR detectors:

● **Temperature**

138. At approximately 30°C PIR detectors become insensitive to intruder movement. At this temperature infrared energy radiated by a human is very similar to background radiation and accordingly the device cannot perceive the movements of a human. PIR detectors incorporating temperature compensation simply set the device to maximum sensitivity at human body surface temperature. Set in this mode of maximum sensitivity the device is assisted in its detection of human movements by the fact that different parts of the human body have slightly different surface temperatures. However there still needs to be a temperature differential of at least 2°C to be confident of movement detection.

● **Relative humidity.**

139. PIR detectors have a good tolerance to humidity variation. In fact, the principle of operation is virtually unaffected by humidity. However at relative humidity below 10% and above 90% problems are likely to occur. This is primarily due to the reactions of the processing circuitry where lack of humidity may allow static

Fig. 6.   Ceiling mounted PIR detectors

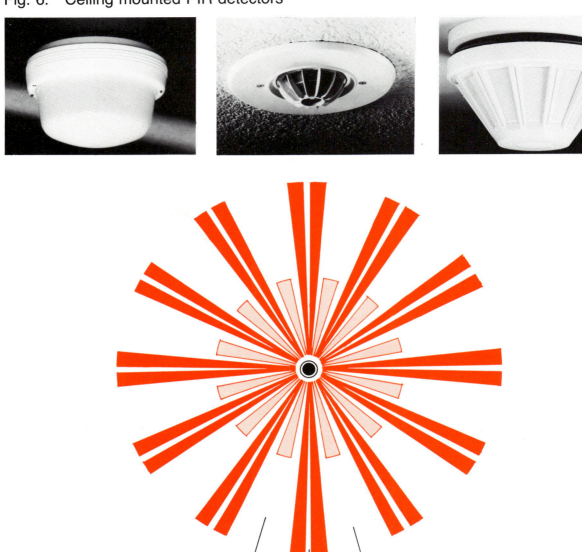

Plan view of full 360° coverage pattern.

15°   0°   15°

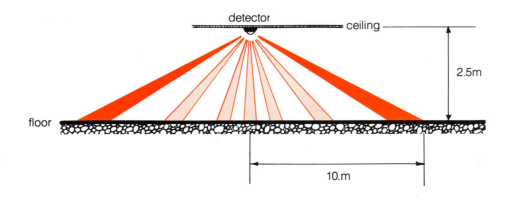

detector   ceiling

2.5m

floor

10.m

Side view of 360° coverage pattern.

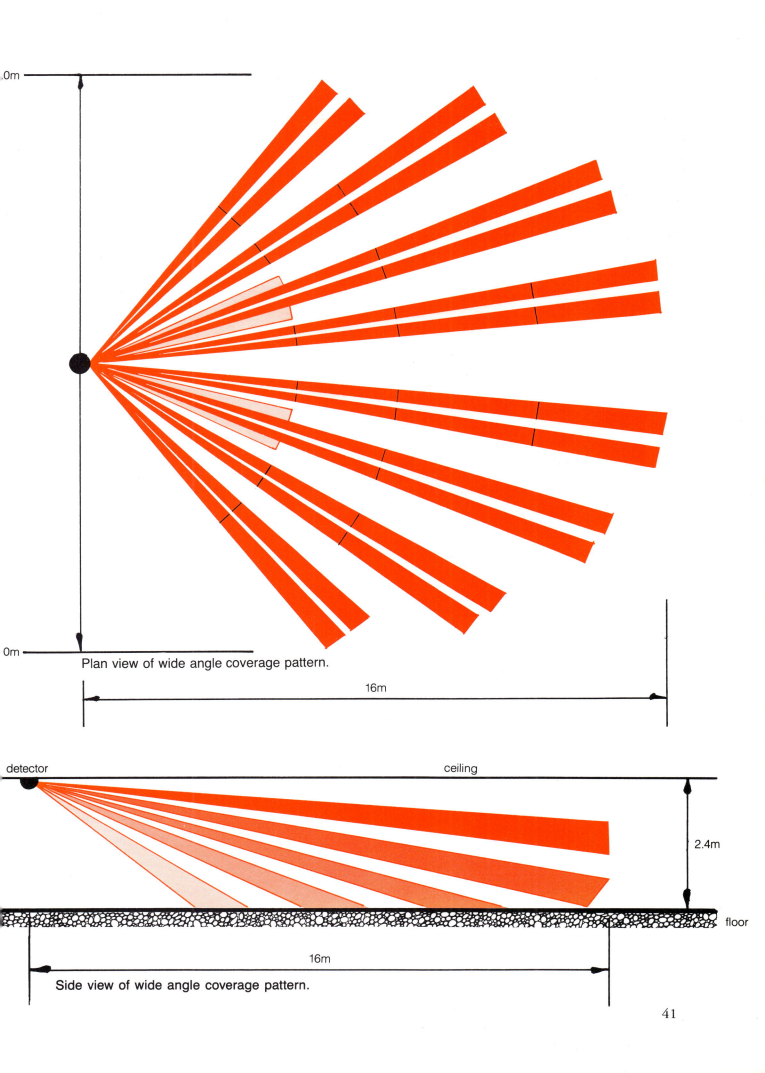

0m

0m

Plan view of wide angle coverage pattern.

16m

detector

ceiling

2.4m

floor

16m

Side view of wide angle coverage pattern.

41

(Figure 6 continued)

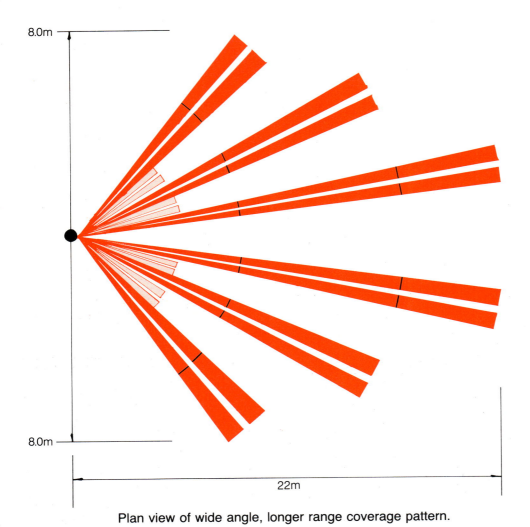

8.0m

8.0m

22m

Plan view of wide angle, longer range coverage pattern.

detector

ceiling

2.4

floor

22m

Side view of wide angle, longer range coverage pattern.

42

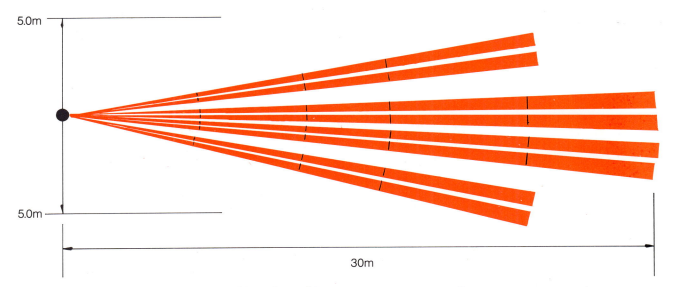

Plan view of long range coverage pattern.

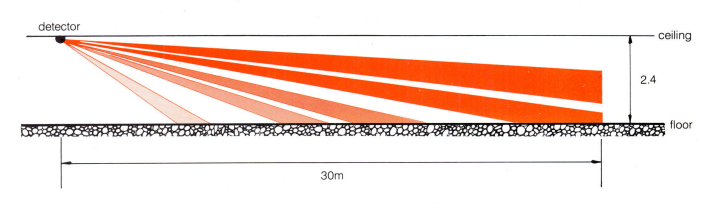

Side view of long range coverage pattern.

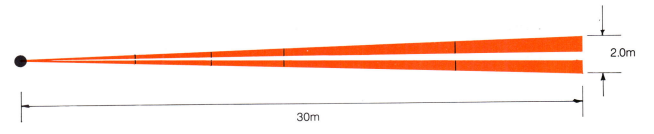

Plan view of vertical curtain long range coverage pattern.

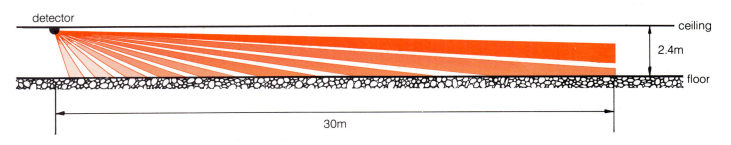

Side view of vertical curtain long range coverage pattern.

43

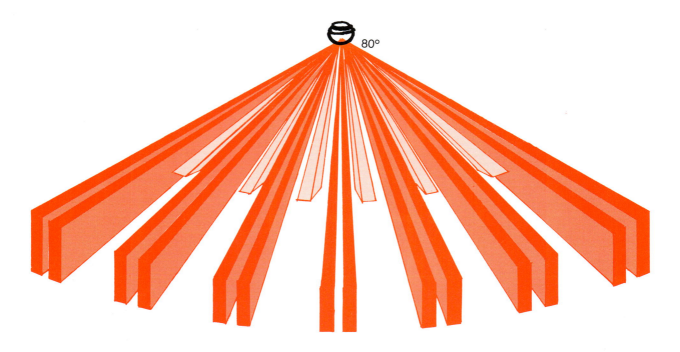

Isometric view of wide angle coverage pattern.

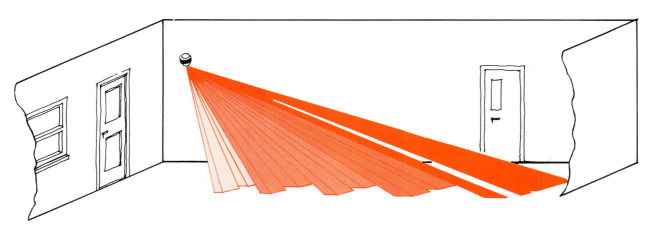

View of curtain type coverage pattern.

44

electricity to build up and high levels of humidity may cause moisture to have an effect on the processing circuitry.

140. The optics of the device will become obscured if condensation forms upon the lens or the lens cover.

● **Air motion.**

141. PIR detectors are not directly affected by air movement. However if air strikes the surface of an object within the field of view, causing a sudden slight change of surface temperature, a false alarm may be activated. Similarly air movement directly upon the detector may cause an alarm condition. Also glass windows may sustain a small, but rapid change in temperature due to beams of sunlight being broken by swaying trees.

● **Light.**

142. Variation in ambient lighting levels is unlikely to activate a PIR detector. However, Tungsten halogen floodlighting and car headlights can impose a temperature change upon the sensor that may activate an alarm if directed into the lens of a detector. Detectors with inadequate false alarm immunity may be activated by ordinary tungsten light bulbs.

143. Sunlight may also activate a false alarm when it penetrates directly into the detector. At certain times of the year the sun appears very low in the sky and may easily penetrate through a window and into the lens of a detector. In exceptional circumstances sunlight may be reflected from a polished floor and into a detector since generally the zones of protection radiate from the detector at an angle towards the floor. Dual element, or quad, detectors have good immunity to light activated false alarms, and are suited for schoool applications particularly where glazing is extensive.

● **Heaters and radiators.**

144. Avoid directing the detector at any source of heat. There have been many false alarm activations caused by heaters switching on automatically prior to building occupancy. In some instances the air turbulence created by heat can cause objects to move thereby producing a change in background radiation which may possibly produce a false alarm. Christmas decorations and hanging mobiles are typical examples.

● **Insecticides**

145. Ensure that the detector is positioned to avoid the lens or cover being sprayed by liquid fly killer or other insecticides.

● **Physical objects**

146. The PIR detector's zones of protection do not penetrate glass or other physical objects. Accordingly such objects may form a barrier behind which an intruder may pass undetected. However, in practice, with optical lenses producing a dense pattern of coverage, it would be extremely difficult for an intruder to pass between solid objects within the field of coverage without the alarm activating.

Commissioning notes

147. Unlike microwave or ultrasonic detectors the early PIR devices were not fitted with a sensitivity adjustment. Since glass and other building materials form an impervious barrier to the range of a PIR detector sensitivity is not an important consideration when determining the effects of external environmental factors. However, some of the much more sensitive modern PIR detectors have a sensitivity adjustment and this must be carefully set so as to be in harmony with its environment. If the detector is set too sensitive it may activate in response to a cool draught, slightly cooling the surface of an object within the field of coverage. Conversely, lack of sensitivity may permit a careful intruder to pass undetected. An apt trade expression, refers to PIR detectors as "going to sleep" in warm environments. Accordingly, when walk testing to check sensitivity levels, it must be realised that the device will probably be far more sensitive on a cold winter's night than on a hot summer's afternoon. Hence the actual commissioning environment must be compared with the variances of actual operating conditions when the setting of the sensitivity control is determined. Some detectors have the advantage of mobile optics that can be moved into position to enable the pattern of coverage to be confirmed by displaying a light that is only visible from points within the field of coverage.

148. Proprietary test meters may aid setting of sensitivity. Also some detectors incorporate an LED circuit that indicates high levels of background disturbance necessitating a reduced sensitivity adjustment. As a rule of thumb, background disturbance should not account for more than 30% of the alarm threshold value.

149. Heating, ventilation and lighting is often

automatically controlled and may come on prior to building occupancy. This results in rapid environmental changes which could create a false alarm condition. Where possible such adverse environmental conditions should be simulated during commissioning. Failing this, sensitivity controls should be set to compensate where possible.

150. Refer to commissioning as detailed within section 4.

151. Figures 4, 5 and 6 illustrate coverage patterns for the various types of PIR detectors.

DUAL TECHNOLOGY DETECTORS

152. These movement detectors contain two separate, interconnected, devices within the same housing. A PIR device is normally combined with another device such as an ultrasonic or microwave movement sensor.

153. Dual technology detectors are primarily intended for use in environments where occasional high levels of background environmental disturbance constitute an exceptional false alarm risk. Before an alarm signal can be activated both of the two separate technology devices must sense an alarm condition, either simultaneously or within a defined time lapse. Since PIR devices respond to temperature change occurring due to the motion of an intruder and both microwave and ultrasonic devices respond to actual physical motion, the two separate technologies have different sensitivity levels to different environmental disturbances. Consequently, random factors that may activate one technology will not stimulate the other technology. For example, fast moving headlights may activate a PIR device, but neither ultrasonic or microwave technology will sense the presence of any motion, accordingly a false alarm will not be activated.

154. Since two separate technologies are used in a combined detector both of these can be used in a highly sensitive mode. By way of an illustration, a basic stand alone microwave detector may seek a doppler frequency shift of approximately 100 hertz or more which equates to walking speed, whilst when this device is employed as one of the technologies of a dual technology combination, the microwave sensor may be designed to produce an alarm condition for a doppler frequency as low as 10 hertz. Although such a high level of microwave sensitivity could be highly reactive to random environmental factors, it is very unlikely that the same random factors would cause the PIR device to activate, accordingly a false alarm would not arise.

155. Two types of dual technology detectors are commonly available. Either the PIR combined with an ultrasonic detector or a PIR combined with a microwave detector.

156. In comparison to the PIR/microwave combination, the PIR/ultrasonic arrangement has a greater coincidence of susceptibility to common environmental disturbances, resulting in a higher false alarm risk. In practice, however, this combination can be used to excellent effect in most difficult environments. The coincidence of both PIR and ultrasonic technologies simultaneously producing a false alarm can be virtually eliminated by employing a PIR section incorporating double element or "quad" sensor arrangements, backed up by high levels of circuit processing.

157. The adoption of two separate devices of different technology greatly increases the component parts of the device. Accordingly the likelihood of the detector failing, particularly the active components, is considerably more probable than in the case of the single technology device. A separate walk test light should confirm the operation of each technology. Ideally, another light will indicate when a pre set ratio in the number of activations of each technology is exceeded during the disarmed period, thereby giving early warning of one device being either over or under sensitive.

158. In view of the advances that have been incorporated in stand alone PIR and also ultrasonic detectors to achieve high levels of fales alarm immunity, the viability of using the more expensive dual technology devices needs to be carefully analysed. There is a strong opinion that single technology offers higher levels of security than dual technology. However in the most adverse environmental conditions, dual technology detectors have a valuable role to play. Lightweight buildings such as portable classrooms situated in exposed locations are just one possible application. Even dual technology devices have their limitations, in an extremely adverse environment at least one technology is likely to be in an almost permanent alarm mode thereby reducing the device to that of single technology.

159. Dual technology detectors generally impose a greater electrical current demand on the alarm system and as a consequence this increases the voltage drop on cable runs. When a dual technology detector is used to replace a single technology detector because of persistent false alarm activation, care should be taken that any additional current demand imposed upon the system will not give rise to an unacceptable increase in voltage drop.

160. The PIR/ultrasonic combination generally has a broad pattern of coverage extending up to a maximum of about 10m. PIR/microwave combinations have various options regarding the field of coverage, including long range to a distance of approximately 60m.

161. As a rule of thumb, dual technology detectors are approximately 2-2½ times more expensive than single technology devices.

162. To more fully appreciate the nature of dual technology detectors it is necessary to gain an understanding of each of the separate technologies of PIR, ultrasonic, and microwave. Before specifying any particular dual technology detector, careful attention should be given to the manufacturer's performance specification, particularly with regard to levels of sensitivity.

163. A guide to detector requirements and environmental considerations may be assessed from the descriptive text herein regarding each of the separate technologies.

164. Walk testing assumes a position of prime importance with dual technology detectors. It is important to create motion separately in radial and lateral directions through the entire field of coverage, both in close proximity and also at the edge of the intended field of coverage. An alarm should be activated in all areas of the required field of coverage by motion typical of that created by a slowly moving, cautious intruder. Figure 7 illustrates typical coverage patterns for dual technology detectors.

SELF-MONITORING DETECTORS

165. At the date of this publication, detector manufacturers are seeking to produce a full range of self-monitoring detectors. Active detectors, such as the ultrasonic device, lend themselves to this self-monitoring function since the device inherently monitors its own self-generated signal. To simulate this principle in the PIR detector an active infrared transmitter is added, for producing an infrared aura for the passive sensor to monitor. Protection is also provided against attempts to 'blind' the PIR sensor.

PRESSURE MATS

166. Pressure mats are intended to be hidden under carpets and will activate an alarm when subjected to foot pressure. They are manufactured in a large range of sizes with the smallest 150mm by 600mm mat intended for insertion under a stair carpet.

Fig. 8   Typical pressure mat.

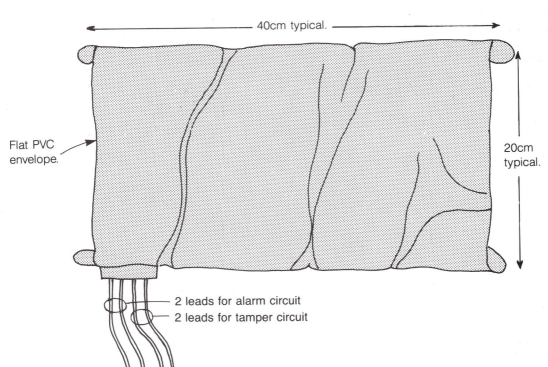

40cm typical.

Flat PVC envelope.

20cm typical.

2 leads for alarm circuit
2 leads for tamper circuit

Fig. 7   Dual technology detectors.

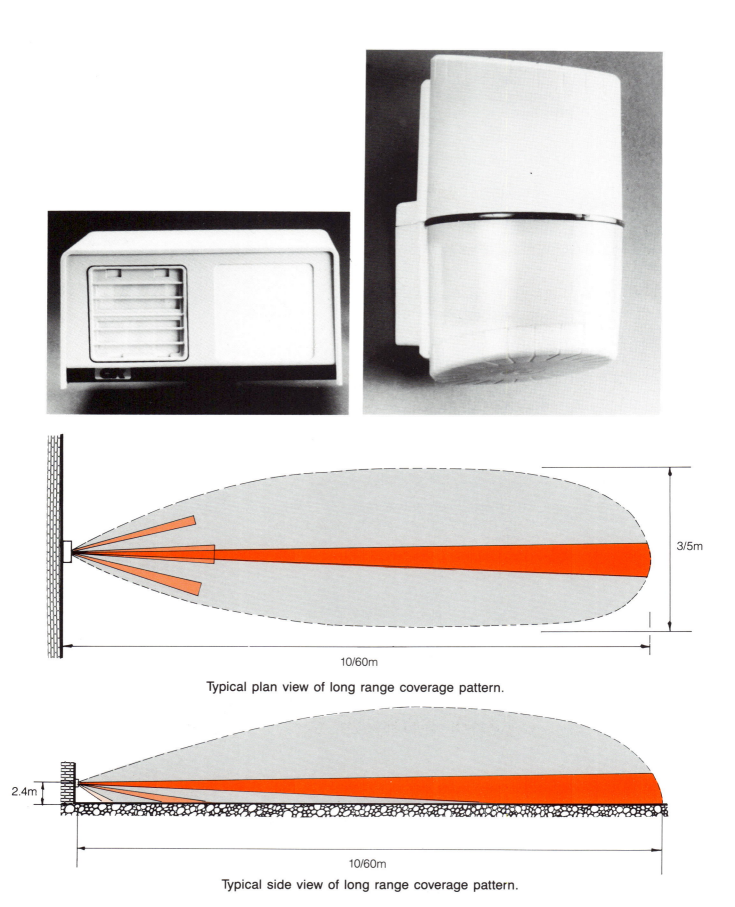

Typical plan view of long range coverage pattern.

Typical side view of long range coverage pattern.

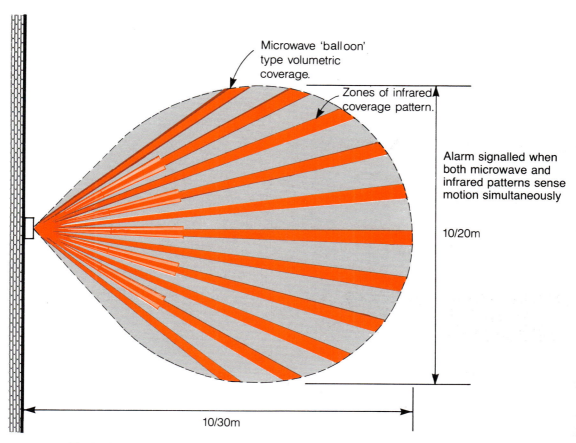

Microwave 'balloon' type volumetric coverage.

Zones of infrared coverage pattern.

Alarm signalled when both microwave and infrared patterns sense motion simultaneously

10/20m

10/30m

Typical plan view of wide angle coverage pattern.

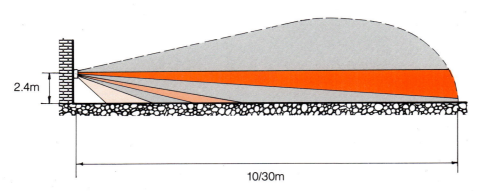

2.4m

10/30m

Typical side view of wide angle coverage pattern.

Note: Ranges vary according to different manufacturers models.

Modern pressure mats consist of a very thin PVC envelope containing a sandwich arrangement of two thin metallic foil sheets separated by a thin sheet of foam rubber. A pattern of holes in the foam permits the foil sheets to establish an electrical contact under foot pressure. The foam is sufficiently spongy to separate the contacts upon release of foot pressure.

167. Protruding from the envelope are four fly lead connections. Two are connected to the metallic foil sheet and carry the alarm signal. The remaining two leads form the ends of a continuous wiring loop within the PVC envelope. Since the foot pressure of an intruder is used to "make" an electrical contact, pressure mats have a security weakness since under fault conditions the mat could fail permanently in the "non-alarm" mode. Accordingly regular testing is essential, particularly where mats are placed in areas with heavy foot traffic during periods of normal occupancy.

168. The pressure mat needs to be carefully concealed under the carpet to be completely unobtrusive and at the same time strategically placed for maximum likelihood of trapping the intruder. If this criterion can be fully met with the mat positioned in an area away from normal occupancy foot traffic, there is the added advantage of less physical wear upon the pressure mat and less likelihood of the mat outline becoming distinguishable from above the carpet. Pressure mats are not intended to be installed beneath plastic floor coverings.

169. Dampness can have an extremely adverse effect. If moisture penetrates inside a pressure mat there is a likelihood of false alarms or of a failure to repond to alarms situations. Avoid siting pressure mats where footwear may deposit rain water or snow.

170. Figure 8 shows a typical flat PVC envelope type pressure mat, with fly leads for protective and tamper connections.

171. In determining the location of a pressure mat consideration must be given to the proposed cable wiring route. With this in mind there is an advantage in siting the mat close to a wall or doorway where the cable can subsequently be routed to an adjacent wall and thereby concealed from view.

172. At the date of this publication pressure mats may be purchased for less than £2. With the greater availability of reliable electronic movement detection there has been a decline in the use of pressure mats. They have limited scope for school applications.

173. Further requirements for pressure mats are detailed in BS 4737: Part 3

PROTECTIVE SWITCHES

174. Protective switches are normally concealed in doors and window frames and activate an alarm, when a magnet fixed to the top of the door or window is moved due to the opening of the door or window. With a purchase price of less than £2 they offer a reliable cost-effective form of protection. With determined effort they can sometimes be disabled and accordingly protective switches cannot normally be regarded as high security devices. However they adequately meet the needs of most school building applications. In trade literature they may be referred to as magnetic reed contacts (MRC) devices.

175. Protective switches have had a long history in security applications and a number of technical variations have evolved. However for all practical purposes the present industry standard can be regarded as the magnetic contact protective switch. The simplicity of this device provides long-term reliability without false alarms. However this is not achievable when poor quality protective switches are employed or standards of installation practice are inadequate.

Design and operation of protective switches

176. Two types of protective switch are commonly available, either concealed or surface fixed, the mode of operation is identical. At the heart of the device is a reed switch consisting of two springy, reed-like wires, having contacts at their ends. Under the influence of a magnet the contacts can be made to touch or separate, thus activating an alarm when a magnet fixed in a door or window is moved. To reduce contact resistance the reed switch contacts should be plated in Rhodium or silver. Degradation of the switch is further reduced by encapsulating the reed assembly in an airtight envelope which is subsequently pressurised with an inert gas. Finally the device is enclosed in a protective plastic or aluminium enclosure. The use of separate ferrous metal screening around the protective switch can be used to combat attempts to disable the device by placing a magnet close to the protective switch.

177. In the most likely application, the protective switch will be installed in the top member of a door frame. In conjunction with this a permanent

magnet will be concealed into the top of the door head coordinated to marry up to the face of the protective switch when the door is in the closed position. Under the influence of the magnetic field the alarm contact reeds are held together forming a closed circuit. Opening of the door removes the magnetic field allowing the reed contacts to spring apart thus producing an open circuit which activates the alarm signal. This mode of operation has a security advantage since the device is most likely to fail into the alarm condition.

178. To facilitate connections to the alarm system wiring, the protective switch is provided with either four terminals or a four-core fly lead. Two connections provide the alarm circuit whilst the remaining two are the ends of a tamper loop inside the switch.

Installation of protective switches

179. The installation must adhere to certain basic requirements to effect good levels of security without false alarms. A protective switch can be most effective when it is concealed in a door frame and fully hidden from view. The installer needs to apply skill in cutting the holes and discreetly concealing the device together with its associated wiring. This latter point is particularly important since visible wiring can draw attention of an intending intruder to the fact that a door or area is protected. Whenever possible the wiring should be concealed, but where any needs to be surface run it should be on the side least likely to be noticed. It should also be adequately protected to minimise the possibility of anybody tampering with it at any time.

180. Of prime importance is the relative position of the protective switch and its operating magnet. Accurate alignment is most essential. The gap between the magnet and the face of the protective switch should not normally exceed 0.5cm except where a special long gap device is used permitting a gap up to 2.5cm. Where an excessive gap exists the magnetic field acting upon the reeds will be weakened and may fail to keep the reeds in contact when environmental factors cause slight vibrations or movement of the door. The protective switch and its associated magnet must be compatible, therefore

Fig. 9   Concealed protective switch typical application.

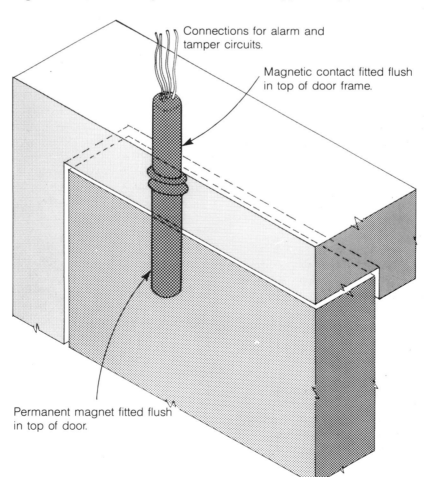

Connections for alarm and tamper circuits.

Magnetic contact fitted flush in top of door frame.

Permanent magnet fitted flush in top of door.

Fig. 10 Surface mounted protective switch typical application.

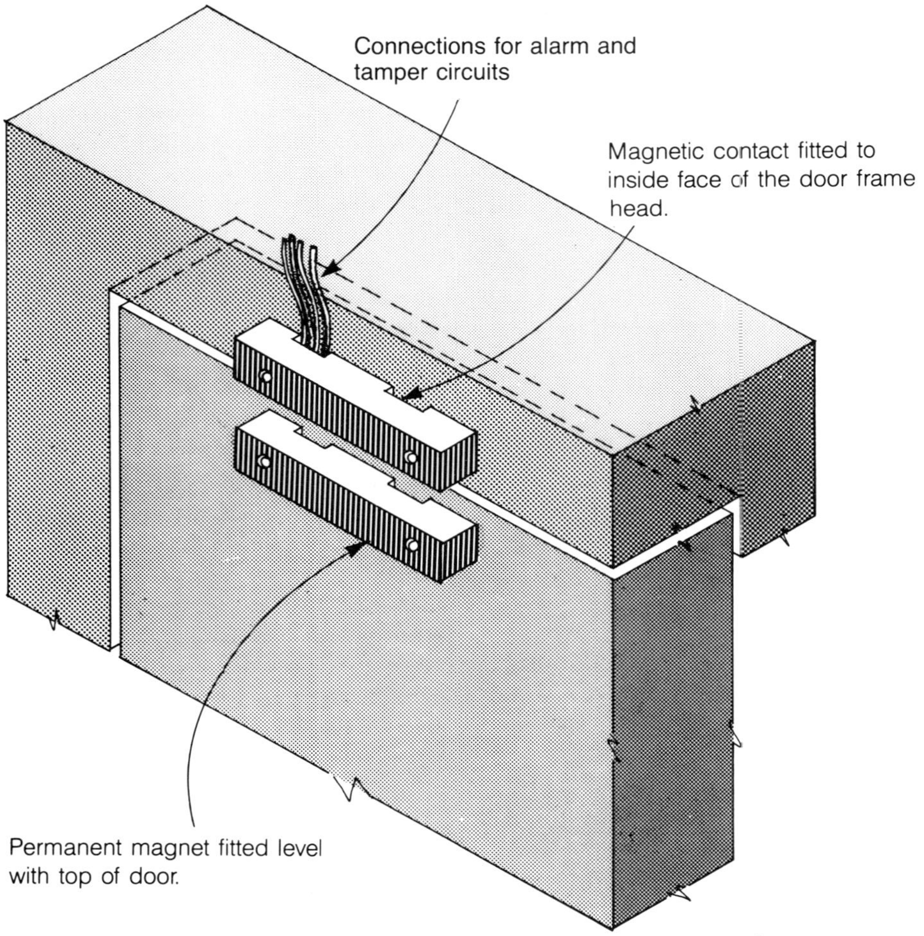

Connections for alarm and
tamper circuits

Magnetic contact fitted to
inside face of the door frame
head.

Permanent magnet fitted level
with top of door.

it is essential that the magnet is matched to the
particular protective switch. Inadequate magnetic
force will result in false alarms; conversely too much
magnetic force may not permit the reeds to separate
when the door has been opened sufficiently to
permit access to an intruder.

181. For schools, the most suitable location for a
· protective switch is when it is concealed in the head
of a door frame, approximately 200mm distant from
the hinge side. This will permit draught movement
of the door, on its catch, or non-malicious attempts
to open the door without raising a false alarm.
However the protective switch will still be sensitive
enough to activate an alarm before an opening of
any significance occurs. Exceptionally where internal
doors are securely aligned in their frames, the
protective switch may advantageously be sited
nearer to the opening edge. BS 4737 requires that
the device operates before the opening exceeds
100mm. Any remedial work needed to the door
should be carried out prior to the alignment of the
magnet with the protective switch. For schools it is
not generally recommended to fit protective
switches to the vertical members of a door frame.

The protective switch would lack sensitivity on the
hinge side and present an unacceptable false alarm
risk on the catch side, unless the door is in good
alignment and securely held when locked. It is
important that any opening fitted with a protective
switch incorporates a properly maintained latch or
other mechanical device to hold the opening in the
closed position thereby preventing accidental false
alarms. **Where locks or bolts are used it is
necessary to ensure that fire regulations are not
infringed.**

182. In certain applications, surface-mounted
protective switches are the only option. Often this
applies to metal doors and windows. To reduce
risks of vandal damage and identification by the
potential intruder, surface-mounted devices should
be installed in as neat and unobtrusive manner as
possible. Towards this aim, some manufacturers
offer a choice of colour.

183. Protective switches are virtually maintenance
free and have a long life expectancy. Eventually, the
reeds may fail or the permanent magnet may grow

weak. Sometimes a loose door hinge or faulty catch will produce a false alarm.

184. During commissioning, the door or other opening section should be moved within the limit of its securing mechanism to ensure that an alarm cannot be induced. This is particularly relevant with metal fixtures since the magnetic field may be reduced in strength. Commissioning tests should also ensure that an opening of 100mm cannot be exceeded before the device operates.

185. Protective switches are manufactured for some specialist applications including protection to roller shutter doors.

186. Figures 9 and 10 illustrate typical applications for concealed and surface type protective switches.

187. Further requirements for protective switches are detailed in BS 4737: Part 3:

CONTINUOUS WIRING

188. Continuous wiring, in tubes, is most effectively used to protect against intruders gaining entry through small windows or roof lights. Small diameter metal tubes, of a maximum 1 m length, are fixed across the opening at maximum spacings of 100mm. The system of wiring passed through the tubes consists of an interwoven circuit configuration of two closed loops. If either loop breaks, or makes shot circuit contact with the other loop an alarm is activated. This once commonly used form of protection has fallen into decline as volumetric devices have taken precedence. However, continuous wiring in tubes can be effectively used in many applications and also where volumetric protection is installed as the main form of intruder detection.

189. Although inexpensive in material content, the labour-intensive task of fixing and wiring the tubes may raise its installation cost to that of volumetric protection. The most cost-effective applications are where small windows or roof lights exist in highly compartmentalised spaces. Typically, a catering block may be constructed with a flat roof and partitioned into small stores, food preparation, cooking, washing-up, office and corridor spaces. Here, continuous wiring in tubes may be cost-effective in protecting the small stores and other spaces which typically are provided with small windows or roof lights. This form of protection acts

Fig. 11   Continuous wiring in tubes typical application.

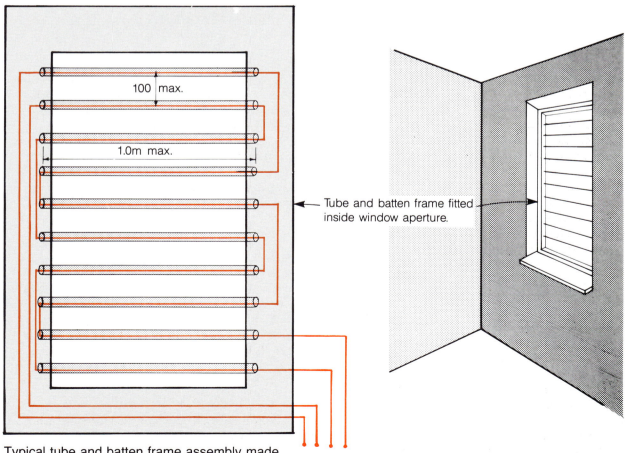

100 max.

1.0m max.

Tube and batten frame fitted inside window aperture.

Typical tube and batten frame assembly made to size of window aperture.

as a visual deterrent to the casual intruder and provides a signal at the first instant of an attempted break-in. Furthermore, immunity exists against the environmental factors that adversely affect volumetric protection. Unlike volumetric methods of protection there are no electricity consuming components and advantageously this method of protection will not impose a voltage drop on the alarm system wiring. This may be a benefit when it is necessary to economically extend protection to a remote part of a school building, or to any part of a system that cannot support further electrical loading without supplementary power supplies. This method is relatively accessible and is susceptible to physical damage, accordingly it is unlikely to be effective when installed in areas of school pupil occupancy.

190. Continuous wiring in tubes does not in itself offer high levels of security. With effort, it may be disabled by an intruder possessing knowledge of the electrical connections. Accordingly volumetric or other forms of protection should be provided to protect against an intruder penetrating further into the building.

191. Tubes across windows are generally aesthetically unacceptable for normally occupied spaces and in some situations may even obstruct the fire escape route. An alternative similar method of protection dispenses with the use of tubes. This form of continuous wiring suffers greater exposure to accidental damage and is unlikely to be suitable for use in schools.

192. Figure 11 shows continuous wiring in tubes mounted to a frame fixed inside a window opening.

193. For further details of continuous wiring protection refer to BS 4737: Part 3.

FOIL ON GLASS

194. This traditional form of protection consists of very thin aluminium or lead tape bonded near to the edges of a pane of glass. When the glass is cracked or broken the tape will break and activate an alarm. Where two adjacent tapes are applied in a double pole circuit arrangement, an alarm will also be activated if the two tapes make contact with each other. The tape is specifically manufactured to break easily when the glass is broken and to achieve this degree of fragility its maximum permissible dimensions are 0.04mm thick and 12.5mm wide. Consequently the tape has very little resistance to

accidental damage and therefore great care must be taken in the installation process. Thorough preparation is essential and in respect of this the glass must be clean and free from condensation and grease. The tape should not be fixed to plastic film. BS 4737: Part 3, details examples of permissible locations for foil.

195. One of the most commonly used arrangements for normal plate glass application is where the metallic foil tape is bonded as a continuous closed circuit loop around the perimeter of the glass, with its two ends terminated at a block of terminals fixed near one corner of the pane of glass. To comply with British Standards, the tape must be fixed within a zone 50mm-100mm from the inside edge of the frame. Where higher levels of security are required or simply to facilitate the wiring installation, two tapes may be run in parallel connected at the terminal block to form two separate closed circuits. If either tape is broken, or if the tapes touch, an alarm will be activated.

196. The foil tape should be firmly bonded to the glass as one continuous length, necessitating the corners to be carefully folded over, creating a 45° crease. Before the widespread use of self-adhesive aluminium foil tape, this tape was bonded to the glass with varnish and then subsequently revarnished to provide a protective covering. By the same principle, the self-adhesive aluminium tape should be sealed with a top coat of non-corrosive transparent lacquer. This will guard against accidental damage without significantly adding to the strength of the tape and thereby reducing levels of security. Most accidental damage emanates from window cleaning activities. It is possible for very fine breaks to occur in the tape, producing random false alarms as wind, temperature and other environmental factors play upon the glass. For schools this method of protection is not recommended for teaching areas or other places of pupil occupancy.

197. The foil tape must not be applied across joins or cracks in the glass. Remedial work should be implemented where the tape becomes detached or blistered. Wired glass, and laminated glass require more extensive treatment of foil tape to effect adequate security than that detailed herein for plate glass. This is because it may be possible to penetrate an area of this type of glass whilst still leaving the perimeter of the glass pane intact.

198. Figure 12 shows a typical arrangement for fixing foil on glass. Examples are based upon recommendations in British Standard 4737: Part 3: Section 3.2.

Fig. 12 Foil on glass.

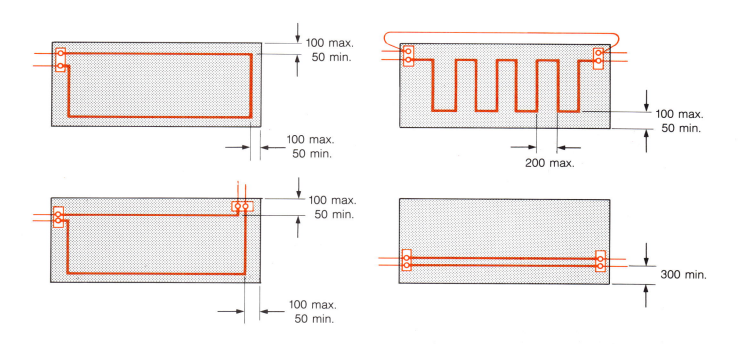

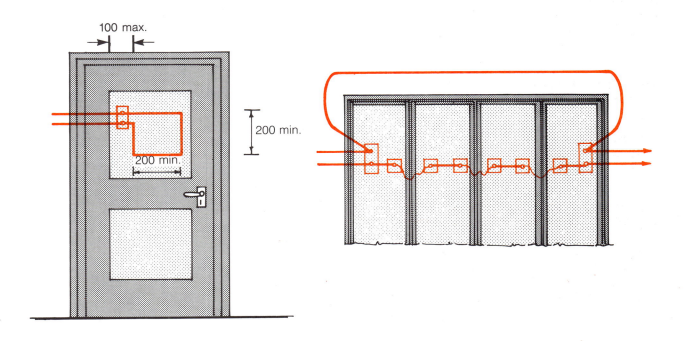

Typical arrangements for foil on glass. Extracts from BS 4737 are reproduced by permission of BSI. Complete copies of the standard can be obtained from them at Linford Wood, Milton Keynes, Bucks. MK14 6LE.

BREAKING GLASS DETECTORS

199. Breaking glass detectors provide a cost-effective form of point of entry protection. There are two types, vibration and acoustic. Vibration devices are bonded to the glass and "feel" the high frequency vibrations, typically 150 kHz, produced when the surface of glass shatters. Acoustic detectors work at audible/ultrasonic sound frequencies and are microphone type devices that "listen" for selected frequency bands of sound that are generated by breaking glass.

200. For multi-pane application acoustic protection is likely to be the more cost-effective. Refer to BS 4737: Part 3 for further information.

201. The following installation and commissioning notes are intended to assist in the appropriate selection of vibration and acoustic types of breaking glass detectors.

Vibration breaking glass detectors

■ Detectors should be fixed close to the edge of a pane of glass. A radius of coverage of 2.5m is normally obtained.

■ These devices are designed for use on standard float glass or plate glass. When used in conjunction with laminated, or toughened glass or where plastic film is applied to the glass, the range of protection will be reduced by at least 50%. They should not be used on wired glass.

■ In order to "feel" the vibrations it is essential that the devices are firmly bonded to the glass. Do not attach to any protective plastic film applied to the glass.

■ The detectors should be protected against the ingress of condensation. Some manufacturers produce waterproof, or totally enclosed detectors.

■ In conjunction with a compatible control panel, these devices may beneficially be connected to a 24 hour zone. This will provide a local alarm if the glass is broken during periods of occupancy.

■ To ensure that a faulty detector fails into the alarm mode the device should be of the normally closed contact type. Connections for a tamper circuit must be provided.

■ The devices will, typically, operate at a frequency of approximately 150 kHz, and incorporate circuit processing to eliminate false alarms from ultrasound and radio frequency interference. Most manufacturers achieve this requirement to excellent effect.

■ These devices normally impose a low current drain upon the system wiring of approximately 10 mA.

■ Vibration devices have excellent tolerance to variations in temperature and may provide satisfactory performance from $-30°C$ to $+70°C$. Variations in levels of humidity are virtually irrelevant where the devices are classified as waterproof.

■ In a school they may usefully be used to protect showcases containing valuable items such as trophies. However it is necessary to ensure that glass is of the standard plate type.

■ Except where urgent security requirements prohibit, the device should be tested in use for a minimum period of 7 days prior to its connection to a remote signalling system.

■ Commissioning should be carried out with the aid of a proprietary tester specifically matched to the vibration detector in use. Such testers are placed against the glass to impose a vibration which simulates that of breaking glass.

■ Detectors should be checked regularly as they may become detached from the glass. Also intruders may gain access by melting a hole in the glass, without producing significant vibrations.

202. Figure 13 shows typical locations for siting vibration breaking glass detectors.

Acoustic breaking glass detectors

■ Acoustic detectors activate an alarm in response to the sound of breaking glass. Since they may operate in the audible/ultrasound range they have a very high natural vulnerability to false alarms being caused by extraneous sound. However, electronic processing can achieve excellent immunity to false alarm activation.

■ Breaking glass produces a very wide frequency spectrum of sound waves. By analysing the wave form produced by breaking plate glass, circuit processing seeks to recognise a defined sequence of relatively low and high bands of frequency at specific amplitudes. Only when sound is generated through this characteristic format will an alarm be activated. Further discrimination is achieved by adding an alarm period. Because the breaking process of glass normally exceeds a period of one second, but lasts less than four seconds, electronic processing is used to eliminate signals of less than one second duration or greater than four seconds duration. The process described here is

Fig. 13 Breaking glass (vibration) detector

Typical applications on standard glass.
(Range may reduce by 50% on laminated or film protected glass.)

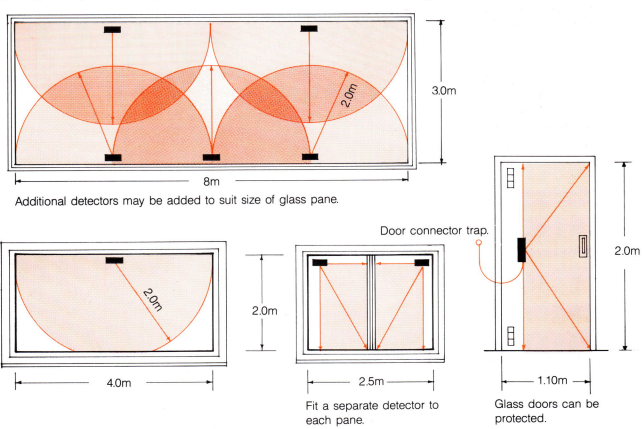

3.0m

2.0m

8m

Additional detectors may be added to suit size of glass pane.

2.0m

4.0m

2.0m

2.5m

Fit a separate detector to
each pane.

Door connector trap.

2.0m

1.10m

Glass doors can be
protected.

typical and manufacturers have developed their own patented variations of circuit processing principles. However, the quality of the signal processing will generally be reflected in the product price.

- Acoustic detectors are suitable for protecting standard plate glass 3-12mm thick but not suitable for toughened or wired glass.

- They may generally be ceiling or wall-mounted up to a maximum range of 5m distance from the furthest points of glass under protection.

- They impose a very low current drain upon the system wiring.

- They can be very cost effective for protecting multi-pane windows, though some acoustic detectors are insensitive to the breakage of very small panes.

- Generally, they possess greater resistance to vandalism than volumetric detectors, particularly when ceiling-mounted.

- Acoustic detectors should be provided with tamper protection and incorporate a latching LED as standard.

- Being a passive device any number of detectors may be used in the same vicinity.

Acoustic detectors should operate within the following environment range.

- Temperature: $-10°C$ to $+50°C$

- Relative humidity: 10% to 90%

- Environmental factors likely to create false alarm risks are as follows:

  - Machinery producing ultrasonic sound

  - Metal to metal contacts such as letter flaps

  - Ultrasonic volumetric detector in close proximity

  - Jets of compressed air or gas

  - Cracked or insecure glass

  - Scratching to the surface of the glass, or glass moving on glazing pins

- A commissioning test should be carried out. Proprietary testers are available but they are generally matched to a particular acoustic device.

203. Figure 14 shows a typical application for acoustic breaking glass detectors.

Fig. 14   Breaking glass (acoustic) detector. Typical application

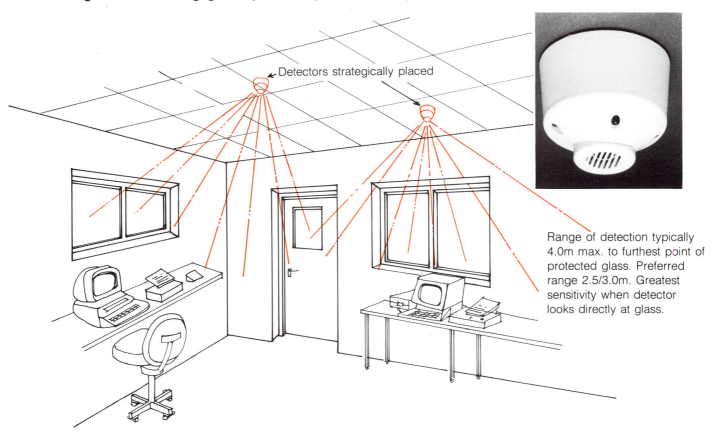

Detectors strategically placed

Range of detection typically 4.0m max. to furthest point of protected glass. Preferred range 2.5/3.0m. Greatest sensitivity when detector looks directly at glass.

Combined technology, breaking glass detectors

204. These detectors incorporate a vibration device together with an acoustic sensor and both must be sensitised to activate an alarm. Unlike single technology devices, combined detectors operate in the lower audible frequency range, typically 1-3 kHz. Since there is less attenuation of sound wavelengths at low frequencies, the range of detection may be as much as 7.5m. This is partly achieved by the fact that each technology can be operated in a highly sensitive mode without serious risks of false alarm.

205. The combined technology device must be firmly secured to a part of the building structure close to, and physically connected to, the window frame. Similarly the glass must be secure in the frame. The vibration sensor "feels" the vibrations that have been produced by the breaking glass and hence transmitted through the building fabric to the point where the device is fixed to the structure. The airborne soundwaves of the breaking glass are simultaneously used to activate the acoustic sensor. When both sensors are simultaneously activated an alarm signal is produced. Draught excluded or hinged windows may not carry vibrations as well as fixed windows, thereby effectively reducing the range of detection.

206. Combined technology devices have a high immunity to false alarms, but these activations may still arise if the glass is subjected to an impact during a period of high ambient noise. Also, vigorous shaking of metal shutters close to the siting of the detector may similarly activate an alarm.

207. During commissioning the device should be tested to ensure that both technologies are functional. Two different testers are used, one produces a safe impact upon the glass and the other generates a sound signal. As with all security devices regular testing is important. This is particularly relevant in the case of combined technology devices. In rare situations, it may be possible for one technology to fall into the non-alarm mode without the building owner being aware of the loss of security protection.

VIBRATION DETECTORS

208. Vibration detectors are fixed to building structures and high security items such as safes and filing cabinets. When attempted entry creates vibration of the sensor an alarm is activated. Most vibration detectors are designed to respond to vibrations characteristic of intruder activity whilst ignoring vibrations from environmental sources. The detectors are tailored to their specific application, which may generally fall into the three categories: general structures, vaults and strongrooms; and single items such as safes and cabinets. There are two types of sensor; electro-mechanical or electronic transducer. Both types are connected to an electronic analyser which may be integral or remote from the sensor. The electro-mechanical sensor is generally defined as an inertia detector. The pure electronic device containing a piezo electric crystal is commonly referred to as a seismic detector.

Vibration detectors for general applications

209. Selection of the correct type of device is imperative. Both inertia and seismic devices are available. In each type of device manufacturers have used ingenious patented analytical processing circuits to discriminate against environmental vibrations, and accordingly performance specifications must be in harmony with application requirements. Where desired protection applies to small numbers of vulnerable items such as doors and window frames, detectors with an integral analyser are most appropriate. Where whole areas of walls, ceilings or floors require protection, groups of up to 8 detectors may be connected to a single, remote analyser. This method is most frequently used in strong room applications. However, for general purpose use, the composite sensor and analyser arrangement is the most commonly used form of protection. Vibration detection provides a first line of defence against intruders. In most applications vibration detection is supplementary to volumetric detection. At the date of publishing, good quality general purpose vibration detectors can be purchased for a sum of less than £20. Figure 15 shows typical applications for general purpose vibration detectors. Refer to BS 4737: Part 3 for further information.

Application notes for vibration detectors

■ Decide upon the principle of detection most suited to the application, either inertia or seismic. Often, either type may be successfully used in general applications. As a rule of thumb, inertia is most appropriately attached to items liable to be rattled or shaken by an intruder's exploratory action. Drilling, levering, cutting and hammering may most appropriately be detected by a piezo electric sensor.

Generally, inertia devices are affected by gravity and accordingly their possible mounting positions are more restricted than those applicable to the piezo electric device which may be universally mounted.

- Whether inertia or piezo electric based, the device must be selected for its analytical circuit processing which should be tailored to the likely forms of attack with immunity to the prevailing environmental vibrations.

- It is necessary to decide if the detector should incorporate a "double knock" feature. This prevents false alarms from single shocks such as that commonly created by a bird colliding with a window. Even in the double knock mode, single shocks of very high intensity or long duration will still activate an alarm.

- The area of coverage may typically extend to a radius of 2.5m under favourable conditions. Hard dense materials transmit vibrations better than soft materials. Also joints between materials may greatly reduce the area of protection.

- A commissioning tool, rather like a spring-loaded centre punch, greatly assists the accurate determination of sensitivity adjustment. However this tool should be specifically intended for use in conjunction with the detector being commissioned.

- The device should be normally closed, with contacts that open to the alarm condition, thus, the vibration detector would fail to the alarm mode.

- In multiple installations, detectors are available with a "first to alarm" LED indication.

- Vibration detectors must be firmly fixed to the surface under protection. Metallic fixing methods transmit vibrations better than plastic or fibre fixings. Vibration detectors can achieve the greatest reliability and areas of coverage when fixed to solid structural components.

- Vibration detectors usually have the advantage of low current consumption generally, about 10 mA.

- The detector should incorporate a tamper protective mechanism, to activate an alarm if the cover is removed or the detector is physically damaged.

- It is necessary to locate sensors away from condensation and direct sunlight.

- The detector should operate satisfactorily in the following environmental range.

  – Temperature: 0°C to 40°C

  – Relative humidity: 10% to 90%

Fig. 15

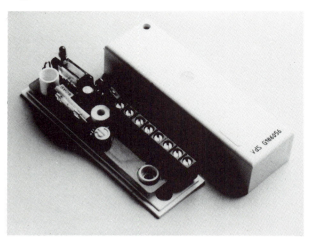

Vibration sensor and processing circuitry, shown with cover removed. Typical dimensions 80mm × 24mm × 20mm.

Typical application to detect attempts to force an entry.

Typical application showing vibration detector and tamper protected door connection loop.

■ In vault and strong room applications up to 8 sensors may normally be connected to one high quality complex analyser, selected for the specific range of possible attacks. The analyser generally provides a separate channel for each sensor with an LED indicator to identify the "first to alarm" sensor and also indicate the condition of each sensor during testing procedures. Predominantly seismic devices are used, but where rattling or shaking motion is guarded against, inertia sensors may be preferable with appropriate matching analysers.

210. For high security, strong room and vault applications, the advice of an experienced specialist is most valuable. Reputable manufacturers will provide the necessary technical support at the design stage.

PROTECTION OF SAFES AND CABINETS

211. Developed from strong room seismic devices, the modern detector specifically for use with safes and cabinets offers high levels of security.

212. The small detectors are mounted on the door or walls of safes. All fixings must be secure and it is recommended that the base plate is either screwed or, preferably, welded to the safe. Tamper-proof junction boxes ease the interconnection of two detectors where tests indicate that both the door and walls require separate detectors. Also, the junction box facilitates the connection of a flexible door wiring loop. Some detectors can be fitted with a swivel plate which can be positioned to cover a keyhole during the alarm set period. Either seismic disturbance or movement of the swivel plate will activate an alarm. This will protect against the insertion of skeleton keys or explosives. Generally, these devices combine the sensor and analyser in one small unit and may be connected direct to the alarm system control panel.

213. Commissioning sensitivity adjustments must be carried out using a proprietary test transmitter specifically designed to match the sensor under test. The most advantageous positions for fixing the sensors for maximum range may be determined prior to installation by the use of a range verification device that is used in conjunction with the test transmitter.

214. Metal is a good carrier of vibrations and detectors fixed to metal surfaces may have an effective range of up to 6m. The extent of this range however will be seriously reduced on other, less dense materials.

215. The above is also applicable to all singular items such as filing cabinets and data storage systems. In this specialist field of security protection the advice of an experienced specialist is of value in determining the most effective form of protection. The requirements of manufacturers installation manuals and performance specifications must be carefully considered prior to the selection of detectors. For maximum protection, the safe should lie within a volumetric detector's field of coverage, which should also be extended along the possible routes of access.

216. Refer to BS 4737: Part 3: Section 3.10.

217. The system should be tested continuously for seven days without producing a false alarm prior to its connection to remote signalling apparatus.

SOUND DETECTORS

218. A forced entry and subsequent intrusion within a building creates noise, the magnitude of which may be hardly discernible to the human ear. Different detectors have been developed for use in general types of building and others specifically for strong room applications. The type used in general building areas predominantly function in the audible frequency range. They have a very high natural susceptibility to false alarms and may be activated by many extraneous factors such as thunder and passing emergency service vehicles. Accordingly they should not be directly connected to any alarm activating controls or signalling apparatus. However, a development of this form of device incorporates a manned control station to which the detector relays, via a telephone line, the signal that activates the alarm. The operator then decides whether or not the sound that originated the alarm, and the subsequently monitored sounds, merit the issue of a full alarm. Window and door contacts can be incorporated to offer a verified form of alarm signal. This unique form of protection can be most effective in combatting the relatively ignorant, noisy, vandal or opportunist intruder.

219. A monitoring and maintenance agreement tied to the installing company is usually necessary.

220. The site installation consists of miniaturised, combined, microphone and amplifier units that are strategically placed throughout the area under protection. Each unit is connected to a local control panel. In the alarm mode, the sound picked up by the active microphone is relayed by the local control to the manned, remote control station.

Fig. 16 Beam detectors

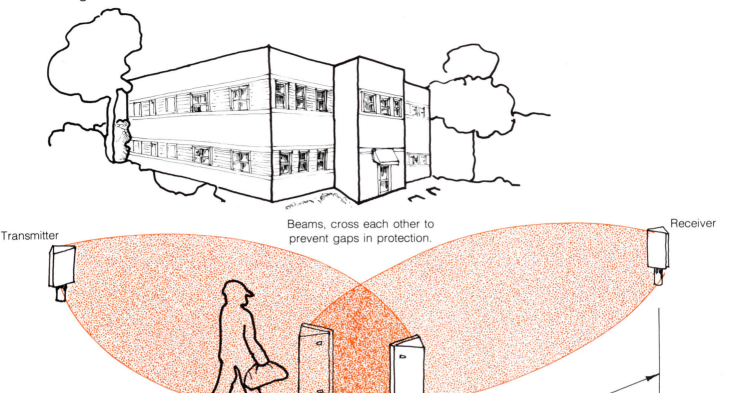

Beams, cross each other to prevent gaps in protection.

Transmitter

Receiver

Transmitter

Receiver

10-200m

Cigar shaped microwave barrier of protection.

221. Although referred to as sound detection, in operation, this type of system may more aptly be described as sound monitoring.

222. Installation and maintenance should be carried out to the general requirements of BS 4737: Part 3. At the time of publishing there is no separate technical British Standard section devoted solely to this type of detection.

223. The sound detectors for use in strongrooms and vaults need to be applied with specialist knowledge. Since they are normally connected to some form of alarm signalling, extensive precautions must be observed to prevent false alarms. As a minimum precaution, a sound meter is used to confirm that the detectors trigger level is at least 15dB above the ambient noise level. They are most effective in strong rooms and vaults where environmental sounds, such as thunder, may not be able to penetrate.

BEAM INTERRUPTION DETECTORS

224. With this type of detector a narrow beam of infrared energy or a cigar-shaped beam of microwave energy is transmitted to an appropriate receiver. When an intruder obstructs the beam falling upon the receiver, an alarm signal is activated. The earliest systems cast an optically filtered beam from a filament lamp. This method had serious reliability limitations rendering it unsuitable for widespread use. With the arrival of solid state components, infrared and microwave systems have vastly extended the application of beam protection. This method of linear protection is most suited to external perimeters and along internal walls, corridors and roofs. Microwave devices are generally intended for external use only, and often referred to as fence or barrier protection. Figure 16 shows typical arrangements for both infrared and microwave installations.

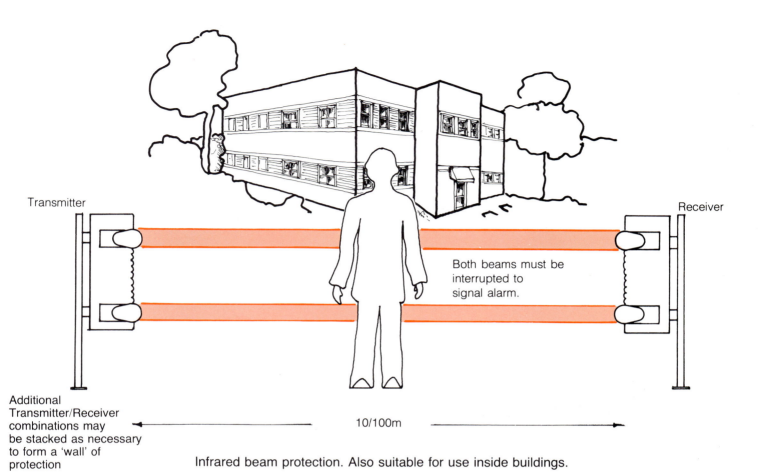

Transmitter

Receiver

Both beams must be
interrupted to
signal alarm.

Additional
Transmitter/Receiver
combinations may
be stacked as necessary
to form a 'wall' of
protection

10/100m

Infrared beam protection. Also suitable for use inside buildings.

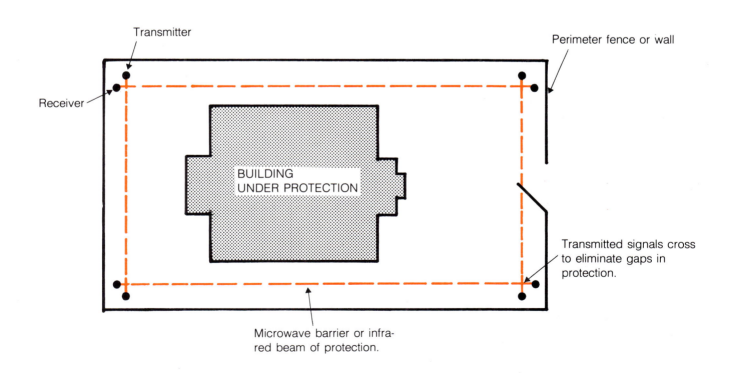

Transmitter

Perimeter fence or wall

Receiver

BUILDING
UNDER PROTECTION

Transmitted signals cross
to eliminate gaps in
protection.

Microwave barrier or infrared beam of protection.

Typical plan of perimeter protection

Infrared beam protection

225. An LED provides the source of infrared energy. The LED output is modulated, pulsed, and transmitted as a narrow infrared beam. The receiver is tuned to match the frequency of the infrared transmitter. Also, the signal processing recognises the frequency of modulation imposed upon the fundamental frequency of transmission. Accordingly, fluorescent and other stray modulating light sources are eliminated as false alarm hazards. Optionally, security levels can be improved where individual matched transmitter and receiver pairs are tuned to an exclusive, confidential frequency of modulation. This prevents the intruder deceiving the receiver by the introduction of a decoy source of infrared radiation.

226. Before the introduction of the high power LED transmitter fog and rain rendered the device unsuitable for external applications. However, in external applications, modulated, high-power transmitters are operated at only one-tenth of their attainable range and therefore have great tolerance to poor visibility weather. Some receivers have the additional feature of issuing an early warning alert when there is a significant reduction in the received signal due to adverse weather. Protection should be provided against condensation which is most often provided in the form of thermostatically controlled integral low power heaters.

227. To form a wall of protection, fence transmitters and their corresponding receivers may be stacked above each other ensuring that the space between the beams is less than human size. Immunity to false alarms from airborne debris and birds can be achieved by connecting the normally closed alarm contacts of adjacent receivers in parallel. Naturally, this increases the size of target that may pass undetected. Some manufacturers produce integral twin-beam transmitter units for use in conjunction with matching twin receivers. Both beams must be simultaneously broken for an alarm condition. Beam projection is difficult to conceal and is readily observed by the intruder who may then seek an alternative route of entry. Detectors are available with obscure covers that do not reveal the direction into which the beam is cast. Circuit wiring should be protected against vandal attack.

228. An extensive range of models exist for both internal and external applications. In respect of this, specifiers should research the market to ascertain the transmitter and receiver combination that is most suitably tailored to the particular application.

229. It is essential that beam systems are mounted to stable fixtures and protected from physical movement. Mounting position must ensure that sunlight cannot directly cast upon the receiver, at any time of the year.

230. Refer to BS 4737: Part 3: Section 3.12.

Microwave beam detectors

231. The antenna of the microwave transmitter directs a beam of electro-magnetic energy to the receiver antenna. The design of the antenna determines the shape of the beam and in most applications a cigar-shaped propagation is used. Typically, the pattern of coverage may extend from ground level to a maximum height of approximately 3m. The range options are generally 30 to 200m distance between transmitter and receiver.

232. Microwaves are inherently radio waves and their behaviour may be comprehended as that surmised by a beam of light, capable of passing through non-dense objects and reflecting off metal objects. Microwave beam detectors sense an alarm condition when the received signal is disturbed by a physical object moving within the beam. Some antennae are deliberately designed to possess greater sensitivity to horizontal movement than vertical motion thereby reducing the risk of false alarms from falling leaves and airborne debris. Present-day systems are predominantly designed for external use and are constructed to withstand all environmental conditions and may sometimes be fitted with low power thermostatically controlled heaters to prevent the formation of condensation. A sensitivity adjustment enables the optimum level of security to be attained.

233. The quality of signal processing is in a constant state of advancement. Digital processing techniques can be used to evaluate the size and speed of the intruder, thereby enhancing immunity to false alarms.

234. BS 4737 refers to intruder alarm systems in buildings, and accordingly, external beam protection is not within the scope of this British Standard. In respect of this, the specifier must determine the technical standard of the proposed apparatus and also ensure good standards of installation practice.

235. External beam detection has evolved from applications in high security establishments such as power stations and oil refineries. In these traditional applications the alarm signal is directed to the on-site security desk. Accordingly any false alarms are contained locally within the establishment. However, with increased criminal activity there is a

trend towards installing external perimeter protection in more general applications. This has instigated the requirement for external protection to be connected to remote signalling apparatus. Prior to the connection of remote signal equipment the approval of the local police should be sought. The police may seek an assurance that every reasonable effort has been made to eliminate the risk of false alarms. It is advantageous to demonstrate that the selected equipment possesses good quality signal processing to provide high levels of false alarm immunity. Similarly, the site installation should be to a high professional standard. Before an external detection system is connected to remote signalling, it should be tested for a minimum period of seven consecutive days without producing a false alarm.

SOME TYPES OF SPECIALIST AND LESS USED FORMS OF INTRUDER DETECTION

236. The following forms of detection are rarely used in schools. However, designers should be aware of these devices and indeed may want to use one or more of them to overcome a particular security problem, or find themselves responsible for the maintenance of existing items.

Capacitive volumetric detection

237. Electrical insulators, including air, possess the physical quality to store an electric charge. For numerical convenience, the amount of electric charge storage capacity is generally measured in units of micro farads.

238. In a closed space with a relatively constant level of humidity and where there is no electrical equipment operating, a reasonably constant level of capacitance prevails in the volume of air in the enclosed space. However, a person entering and moving within this volume of air disturbs the balanced conditions and the capacitance of the volume of the space will rapidly change. Capacitive volumetric detectors are designed to activate an alarm when a person of approximately 60kg moves at walking speed through a distance of 2m.

239. With the advance of other forms in movement detection these devices are very seldom used today and may be adversely affected by humidity and extraneous static electricity.

240. Refer to BS 4737: Part 3: Section 3.8.

241. This form of protection must be operated for a minimum period of 7 days, without producing a false alarm, before its connection to remote signalling apparatus.

Capacitive proximity detectors

242. These devices are most commonly used to protect single items or a small group of items which can be connected together by a single wire.

243. A single wire connects the detector to the protected object. By virtue of this connection the capacitance detector and the protected object achieve a combined balanced, stable level of electrical capacitance. When a person touches or becomes very close to, the protected object a fast rate of electrical discharge occurs resulting in a fast rate of change in the overall level of capacitance. Electronic processing analyses the rate of change and activates an alarm when the rate of change is greater than that which would normally be caused by environmental factors. Although changes in humidity and background static electricity alter apparent levels of capacitance, the change is normally at a low rate and thereby rejected by the processing circuitry.

244. Capacitive proximity detectors are basically intended for connection to metallic objects. However, metallic foil fixed to materials such as wood and plastics, permits successful operation. Typically, the back of a valuable work of art may be screened with a metallic foil that is subsequently connected to a capacitive proximity detector.

245. Refer to BS 4737: Part 3: Section 3.13.

Rigid printed-circuit wiring

246. In this form of protection hard wiring is permanently bonded to rigid panels. A two pole circuit configuration is connected to the alarm system to activate an alarm upon any of the following occurrences:

■ the wiring is cut

■ adjacent wires touch

■ alternative wires touch

■ the wiring is moved more than 50mm.

247. The rigid panels are fitted in position with the hard wiring to the inside of the protected area. It is therefore extremely difficult to tamper with the electrical connections or force an entry without damaging the wiring and thereby activating an alarm.

248. In the wake of advances in electronic methods of protection, this traditional form of protection has virtually fallen into disuse. When correctly installed it has a high immunity to false alarms, but is not suited to damp environments.

249. Refer to BS 4737: Part 3: Section 3.11.

Underground detectors

250. These are activated when a person walks over the detectors. Although various methods have evolved over past years, the hydraulic pressure system is most commonly employed and is extensively used in high security installations such as refineries and power stations.

251. Two fluid tubes run beneath the ground approximately one metre apart. Bleed connection between the two tubes ensures that the system stabilises with the two tubes at equal pressure. When an intruder or vehicle moves across the two tubes a very slight pressure differential is created between the tubes. A highly sensitive pressure sensor will then activate an alarm signal. This system of protection has relatively good immunity to false alarms from small animals and cannot easily be defeated by such methods as placing a plank across the ground above the two tubes. Unlike beam detection this underground method can be satisfactorily used in an area of uneven terrain.

Microphonic cable

252. Such a cable is primarily intended to be routed along and interwoven with chain link fencing, the cable acts as a transducer, converting mechanical vibrations into equivalent electrical signals. In most applications, the cable ends terminate at a control panel situated in an on-site manned security desk. When the fence is cut or climbed, an alarm threshold is exceeded and an alert signal is issued. The audible sound of the attack is reproduced at the security desk, indicating the type of attack. This form of protection is most often referred to by one of a number of proprietary brand names.

New detection techniques

253. Developments in electronics and microprocessor technology will continue to bring forth new methods of intruder detection. Existing forms of sensor will benefit from "intelligence" that will enable the detector to monitor its own technical functioning and also its ambient environmental conditions.

254. The application of laser beams and optical fibre techniques may advance into everyday security applications. Already, optic fibres are employed in hazardous environments where gases, flammable liquids and other corrosive substances render conventional cables inappropriate.

APPENDIX 2   Auxiliary equipment

255. Apart from the main operating components of an intruder alarm system there are other essential parts. These serve to interconnect the entire system and provide for the particular requirement of any scheme.

256. This appendix describes the most commonly used components that may typically be found in any intruder alarm system.

Deliberately operated devices

257. Commonly referred to as panic buttons or personal attack switches they are designed specifically for either hand or foot operation. The devices must be simple to operate but incorporate design features to minimise the risk of accidental operation. Hand operated switches have one or two simultaneously operated buttons, shrouded for protection against unintentional operation. The devices should be fitted with terminals for both alarm and tamper connections.

258. Deliberately operated devices are most likely to be used during periods of building occupancy and should therefore be connected to a control panel possessing a 24-hour armed circuit. To reduce the risk of personal attack upon the user, the device should be fixed in a discreet location requiring a virtual absence of noticeable movement in order for the operator to activate the device.

259. Careful consideration must be given to the signalling mode. In some instances a loud, local audible alarm may pose a greater risk to the person under attack. BS 4737: Part 2 details specific requirements for basic systems and more complex systems incorporating remote signalling. Wire-free systems as detailed further herein, provide for completely portable deliberately operated devices.

Security lock switch

260. This normally consists of a high-quality 5 lever mortice lock into which a switch with change over contacts is fitted. Usually the contacts used are made (unlocked) and open (locked). The switch may be used in the first/final entry door to signal the commencement of an authorised keyholder's entry or completion of an authorised keyholder's exit. When used in systems incorporating remote

signalling, there is a reduced likelihood of false alarms resulting from inadequate entry and exit procedures. The lock switch initiates a pre-set timed entry period enabling the keyholder to enter the premises and walk through a defined entry route to the control panel and hence disarm it without initiating an alarm. Similarly, the lock switch may be used to signal the completion of the exit procedure. The entry and exit routes between the outside and the control panel are normally the same, but it is permissible for them to follow different routes. In basic systems a magnetic contact incorporated in the first/final entry door signals initiation of entry or completion of exit. To place sole reliance on door contacts means that an intruder who attacks this door has the benefit of the timed entry period after activating the door contacts before an alarm is raised. Where a lock switch is used to signal completion of exit, a magnetic door contact can be used to initiate an instant alarm if the door is forced open. This combined treatment of the door can only improve the level of security where the keys to this point of entry are securely kept and not duplicated. Where reliance is placed solely on a magnetic contact, fitted to the door, false alarms may arise from the exit procedure, if the door reopens. The door must be therefore locked in the closed position prior to expiry of the exit time period.

261. In another application, the lock switch is used to temporarily disconnect a section of the protected area where partial occupancy of a building is frequently required. In some schools, holiday period access may be required only to defined areas such as basements, plant rooms and cleaners' stores. Accordingly, the specific areas may be conveniently shunted out by the lock switch whilst the remainder of the school remains protected. There are some schools where high risk portable equipment such as computers and audio equipment are stolen during periods of legitimate occupancy. Where this problem exists it is desirable to protect the individual high risk areas on a 24-hour basis. The protection is only isolated at the actual times of occupancy of each individual computer room or other similar high risk areas. To provide 24 hour protection under local control, the 24-hour alarm loop is used to serve the protected space and is controlled by a shunt lock that is fitted to the room entrance door. The shunt lock should be connected to a proprietary zone omit unit, or similar device, to prevent an isolated area being reconnected whilst it is in alarm mode. The multi-user nature of school

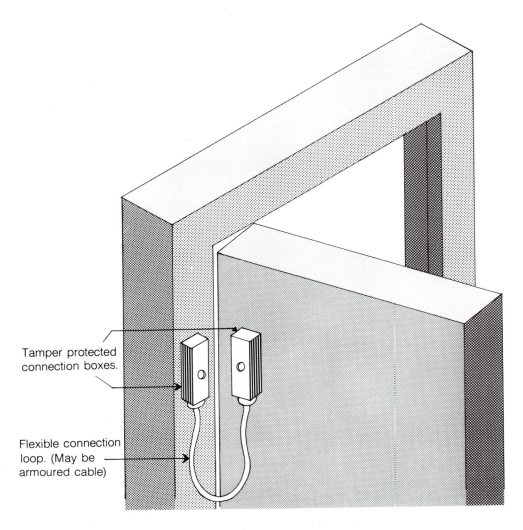

Tamper protected
connection boxes.

Flexible connection
loop. (May be
armoured cable)

Fig. 17   Door connection loop typical application

teaching areas increases the number of persons in charge of access thereby increasing the likelihood of user induced false alarms. As a further move against false alarms, a door contact could be interconnected with the room detector to prevent an alarm activation if the shunt lock is locked closed whilst the door is open.

262. Refer to BS 4737: Section 4.1.

Door connection loops

263. To facilitate flexible connection to devices fitted to openings such as doors and windows, pre-assembled wiring loops are available. They are made from tinsel cable to provide a highly flexible and durable interconnection. Where extendable loops are required, coiled cable, similar to that connected to telephone hand sets, are used. Where vandalism might occur flexible metal sheathed door loops is recommended. At least one LEA has found it necessary to standardise on a highly vandal resistant

armoured door loop of a type that is made to recess into the hinge side of the door frame. These are particularly recommended for connections to the final exit door where a security lock switch is fitted.

264. The interconnection between the door loops and the system hard wiring should be made with tamper protected connection boxes, as shown in Figure 17.

265. Refer to BS 4737: Part 1: paragraph 3.3.5.

Junction boxes

266. For the interconnection of security wiring, appropriate security junction boxes must be used. Any other form of connection box invites the intruder to easily disable the alarm system. Junction boxes should contain contact materials that will not degenerate in the atmosphere and may typically consist of nickel-plated phosphor-bronze. The cover should be impact resistant and designed to activate a tamper signal upon its removal.

PVC cables for interconnecting wiring

267. Cables must be of an adequate cross-sectional area to ensure that the potential difference across the furthest detectors is at least equal to the minimum working voltage stated by the device manufacturer. Ideally, reasonable tolerance should be allowed for further extensions to the system.

268. The most commonly used cable has stranded cores comprising 7, 0.2mm diameter tinned copper conductors. It is generally available in multiples of two cores from 4 to 12 core arrangements. To a lesser extent solid core, telephone type cable is used but its relatively small cross-sectional area imposes a greater system voltage drop, also its single conductor cores are less flexible and may therefore be more susceptible to mechanical damage. Screened or shielded cable can be used to improve physical protection to the cores and also reduce the susceptibility to induced electrical or radio frequency interference.

269. Where environmental conditions prohibit the use of PVC cables, alternative wiring systems should be considered but importance should be attached to cable security and tamper sensitive jointing boxes. MICC cables and other wiring systems, installed in accordance with the latest edition of the **IEE Regulations for Electrical Installations,** may offer suitable solutions.

270. Refer to BS 4737: Part 3

End of lines devices

271. This may refer to a resistor or any electrical component that establishes a potential difference at the point where a circuit apparently terminates.

272. Resistors fitted at the furthest point, or apparent end of individual circuits, can be used to prove a circuit of continuity possessing a defined value of electrical resistance. Thus, if cables are cut or short-circuited a tamper or alarm condition can be activated by a compatible control system.

Batteries

273. Batteries incorporated with, or mounted adjacent to the control panel are used to power the alarm system during periods when the normal electricity supply is unavailable. In the event of an alarm arising during a power breakdown, batteries may be required to power local and remote alarm signalling. The important role of batteries must not be overlooked since the vulnerability to break-ins increases during periods of power failure.

274. The power requirements of the alarm system can be calculated from the technical data of the detection and alarm devices. Accordingly it is possible to determine the ampere-hour rating of the battery necessary to power the system in both armed and alarm mode. BS 4737: Part 1: Para 7.2.1 details an 8hr battery capacity requirement for powering the alarm system in the normal mode. Also the associated charging equipment must restore the charge to the battery within 24hrs.

275. The above text specifically applies to systems incorporating rechargeable batteries. However, other systems utilise a primary battery and here the battery must be capable of sustaining an alarm condition for a minimum period of 4hrs within the service life of the battery. The battery should bear a mark stating the date at which it was installed and regular replacements must be made prior to the expiry of the normal service life of the battery, as stated in the battery manufacturer's instructions.

APPENDIX 3   Wire-free intruder alarm systems and portable alarms

276. In 1986, BS 6799 wire-free intruder alarm systems was issued. Manufacturers have now produced systems in compliance with BS 6799 and they have already been used in some schools where a fully wired system is inappropriate.

277. LEAs have experienced problems with self-contained portable alarm systems but they may help to defend a particular target until a proper alarm system is installed.

278. This appendix describes both wire-free intruder alarm systems and also the stand alone portable alarm.

Wire-free intruder alarm systems

279. This form of intruder alarm system utilises some of the same detection technologies as hard wired systems. Using radio as its communication medium the interconnecting wiring between detectors, local alarms and controls is dispensed with. Small battery powered radio transmitters are either incorporated in the detectors, or fitted adjacent to the detectors. In the event of a detector sensing an alarm condition a radio signal is transmitted to the control receiver which subsequently activates the local audible alarms and any relevant remote signalling equipment.

280. At the time of publishing, many local police forces are reluctant to accept remote signalling calls to attend to premises where wire-free alarm systems are installed. This is largely due to the high levels of false alarms attributable to the poor quality of early imported wire-free alarm systems. Before installing a wire-free alarm system connected to remote signalling equipment, early liaison with the local police crime prevention officer is essential. As a minimum the police are likely to insist that any system fully complies with BS 6799. BS 6799 issued in 1986 defines five categories of wire-free alarm systems. Also the Department of Trade and Industry Radio Regulatory Body has issued transmitter specification requirements. Class IV and Class V have the highest security integrity. Class V systems intercommunicate with each transmitter and report on its input status and battery condition at maximum periods not exceeding 1.2 hours. A Class V system will also activate an alarm signal if a receiver has not had an input from a remote transmitter for a maximum period of 3.6 hours. Class IV systems are required to perform both these functions but within the extended period of a maximum of 8.4 hours. The other three lower classes of system do not possess this level of auto-reporting and thereby have a lower level of security integrity. Since the issue of BS 6799 manufacturers have tended to direct their development effort into producing Class IV and Class V systems for use in fairly large commercial premises. The use of a high gain tuned receiver aerial may permit the system to be extended to a number of building blocks all within reasonably close proximity. Maximum

Fig. 18   Typical school application for a wire-free intruder alarm system.

Combined PIR detector and radio transmitter senses intruder and signals alarm.

VDU store, fitted with door contact and radio transmitter.

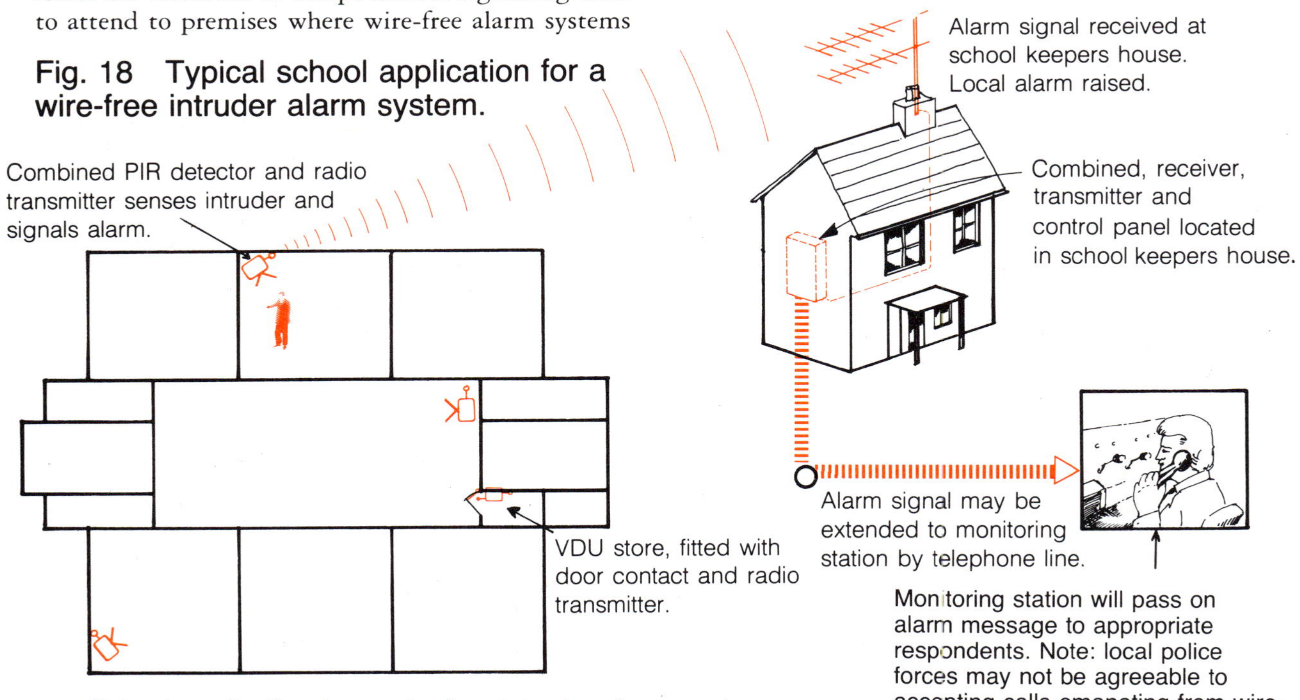

Alarm signal received at school keepers house. Local alarm raised.

Combined, receiver, transmitter and control panel located in school keepers house.

Alarm signal may be extended to monitoring station by telephone line.

Monitoring station will pass on alarm message to appropriate respondents. Note: local police forces may not be agreeable to accepting calls emanating from wire-free alarm systems.

School application for a wire-free intruder alarm system.

transmitter range is attainable when the receiver is fitted with an external high gain tuned aerial. Furthermore, if the detector transmitters are positioned reasonably high above ground level and preferably if they are in line of sight communication with the receiver aerial, maximum communication distances will be achieved. Dense concrete and structural steelwork may seriously reduce attainable transmitter ranges.

281. The importance of regular, frequent auto-reporting cannot be overstated. If a radio transmitter is removed or its battery fails, a security exposure will exist until the control receiver reports that the transmitter has not 'called in' by the periodic time. Hard-wired systems have the advantage of tamper circuits to address the security exposure associated with detectors being deliberately removed.

282. In order to achieve a reasonable service life from batteries, transmitter power and auto-reporting rates have to be limited. Similarly active devices such as ultrasonic detectors require too much power to permit a useful battery life.

283. Specially developed passive infrared detectors contain a transmitter and aerial and also possess the ability to conserve battery energy during the deactivated period by holding the sensor in a quiescent state for a few minutes after each sensor activation. This is particularly relevant in areas of high occupancy levels where the device could be very frequently activated. For exceptional reasons, in some situations, it may be possible to derive a local mains power supply to drive a power pack containing secondary batteries, which themselves can be used to provide a supply to any common form of detector, whilst the transmitter retains its power source from its integral battery.

284. Class IV and Class V wire-free systems offer a very good alternative when a hardwired system is impractical, although it must be remembered that hardwired systems offer the highest levels of security integrity. Wire-free systems have a minimum impact upon the decorations and fabric of the building and may often be installed where the presence of asbestos could prevent a hard wired installation. Compared with hard wired systems they require much less labour for the installation process. However, the transmitters and receiver significantly add to material costs. The need for battery replacement, every six months adds to the maintenance commitment. It is an advantage of wire-free systems that personal attack buttons are truly portable. Diligent commissioning is essential since many unforeseeable factors may adversely affect the ability of the transmitter to communicate with the receiver at the appropriate time.

Commissioning checks should be carried out in conditions relevant to that applying when the system is armed throughout all periods of the year. Actual application experience on the part of the person specifying the system and the engineer installing it is most vital. Interference from natural environmental sources and from electrical plant together with the effects of multi-path reception create considerable problems which the experienced engineer may find reasonably easy to identify and resolve.

285. BS 6799 provides recommendations for the construction and installation of wire-free alarm systems. Explanatory details are provided for each of the 5 categories of wire-free alarm system classification. Figure 18 shows how a wire-free alarm system may be applied to a school site.

Portable alarms

286. Stand alone portable alarm units for space protection generally consist of a movement detector, integral controls, siren, and strobe light. They may scare off the casual opportunist intruder but are easy to physically damage and thus deactivate therefore posing very little deterrent to the experienced criminal. In fact, portable alarms have been stolen along with other items.

287. Some LEAs report that a number of factors make these portable units vulnerable to false alarms, particularly that they are often "aimed" into a volume of space by persons with no technical knowledge in respect of detector sensitivity to environmental factors. The high false alarm risk renders the units unsuitable for remote signalling to the police.

288. Portable alarms can usefully be employed in schools that suddenly become targets for intruders or as a temporary measure in vulnerable buildings pending the installation of a fixed intruder alarm system to BS 4737.

289. A new generation of low cost alarms for bonded attachment to audio-visual equipment and computers can be effectively used where it is necessary to remove equipment from safe protected areas. An ear-piercing sound is emitted when the item is moved and latches into a continuous alarm mode until the system is reset by a key. The difficulties of stealing a video recorder with a loud siren attached to it are self evident.

290. The above text describes typical portable alarm systems. However, there is a considerable number of different proprietary systems available.

APPENDIX 4 Intruder alarm system control panels

291. Intruder alarm system control panels serve as an interface between the different components of the system and the user of the alarm system. They must be selected to be compatible with the extent and technology level of the system. Similarly they must act as a suitable interface to any signalling or monitoring equipment. For schools it is important that the controls are 'user-friendly' to the person who may be new to the alarm system. Figure 19 shows a typical example of modern control panel.

292. This appendix describes the types of available control panels.

293. It was not many years ago that intruder alarm control panels consisted of an assembly of electro-mechanical relays. This relatively simple concept has now fully entered the micro-computer era with some "intelligent" control panels incorporating their own micro-computer. The problem facing today's specifier is the need to select a control panel that is compatible to the pattern of

use of the building into which it is to be installed, yet at the same time, be user friendly and not be too limited or complex for the job in hand. Cost is very much proportional to the degree of technology employed. Essentially, controls must be fully compatible with the types of detection devices, together with their associated remote signalling equipment.

294. The system of wiring and any associated outstations, will generally be installed to suit the type of system dictated by a proprietary control panel. There is no need to describe here all the proprietary types of control systems and associated installation wiring methods available at the date of publication. However, for general guidance a brief description is included detailing traditional wiring for small systems and also a typical large multiplex system. In any type of system, consideration should be given to the almost certain need to expand or reprogramme the system to suit changes in the building's pattern of use.

Fig. 19 Typical arrangement of a modern micro-processor based intruder alarm control panel.

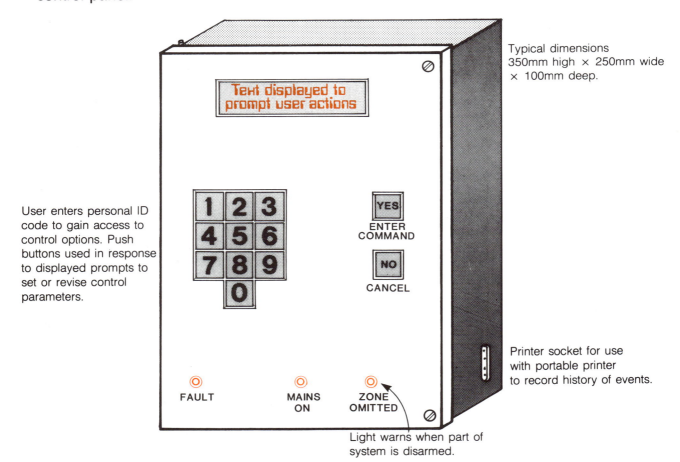

Typical dimensions 350mm high × 250mm wide × 100mm deep.

User enters personal ID code to gain access to control options. Push buttons used in response to displayed prompts to set or revise control parameters.

Printer socket for use with portable printer to record history of events.

Light warns when part of system is disarmed.

295. Under the headings of "small and traditional controls" and "microprocessor based control systems" there are lists of optional operational features. The specifying engineer can draw from the list to assess operational requirements for any project at the embryo stage. The operational requirements thus obtained may be compared against manufacturers' specifications. Figures 20 and 21 show the typical wiring systems for both traditional and microprocessor based systems.

Small and traditional control systems

296. Microprocessor technology is used in a limited form and with most low cost control panels generally a maximum of 6 zones is provided. Outstations for expanding each zone of the sytem are unlikely to be a feature of this limited technology. However, the system possesses all the necessary basic controls and programming options necessary for a satisfactory installation. The installation system of wiring is predominantly of the traditional radial method, separate for each zone.

297. Inside the control panel, input terminals are provided for each zone. Additionally, a nominal 12 volt DC supply is provided by a pair of terminals and two further terminals serve as connections for the tamper loop. Finally, connections are provided for a 24-hour personal attack loop.

298. The traditional method of wiring serves each protected zone by a separate radial circuit. Typically, a 3 pair PVC cable will carry the zone alarm loop, tamper loop, and DC low voltage power supply connecting to each successive detector, on each individual zone. A similar cable serves the local audible alarm.

299. Output terminals are provided for the local audible alarm. One pair of terminals energises the sounder in its alarm mode and another pair provides power to the local audible alarm's integral battery charger. This charging supply may also combine the hold-off function which prevents the sounder being energised by its integral battery whilst the control panel and its charging supply is healthy. Thus, if the cable serving the local audible alarm is cut, the audible alarm will automatically be powered by its integral batteries to sound an immediate alarm. Additionally, a separate latching alarm output may be used to power a strobe light until the controls are reset.

300. There is considerable variance in the features offered by intruder alarm panels of different manufacturers and price range. However, the following list is indicative of minimum basic requirements:

- Terminals provided for entry/exit route with adjustable time delay.

- Part set option leaving one zone only de-activated, for periods of partial occupancy.

- Terminals for connection to digital communicator.

- Test facility enabling deliberate activation of detectors without raising an alarm condition.

- Visual indications of alarmed zone, tamper activation and entry/exit route time overrun.

- Setting arrangements are traditonally by multi-position key switch with a keypad provided on more sophisticated controls.

- Adjustable timer, capable of 20 minutes setting, for use with local audible alarm supply.

- 12/15 volt regulated DC power supply able to discriminate between normal load and charge conditions.

301. For a primary school or other building of similar size, this simple form of control system can be effective and economical. Too much should not be expected since low cost controls often lack the power to drive more than a few movement detectors on any given zone. Similarly, control and programming options may be limited. It is advisable to allow some spare capacity to enable future extensions to the detector circuits. Preferably, at least one spare zone should be allowed.

302. It is essential to compare different manufacturers' specifications to select a control panel of the optimum technological sophistication for the needs of the premises to be protected. Setting and switching off procedures should not be complicated, particularly where temporary staff may find themselves responsible for managing the alarm system controls.

Microprocessor based control systems

303. Microprocessor based control panels extend the capabilities of intruder alarm systems even further. Future technological developments will continue to bring forth new generations of intruder alarm control panels with greater data-processing power and more flexible, user friendly programming procedures. At the date of this publication, multiplex control panels, with keypad programming and operation (setting controls) have proved themselves reliable in service. Programming is carried out in conjunction with a real language written display that asks the user to enter the answers to simple questions. The "intelligent" control panel is a further development with the

Fig. 20 Example of the traditional radial method of wiring with basic type control panels.

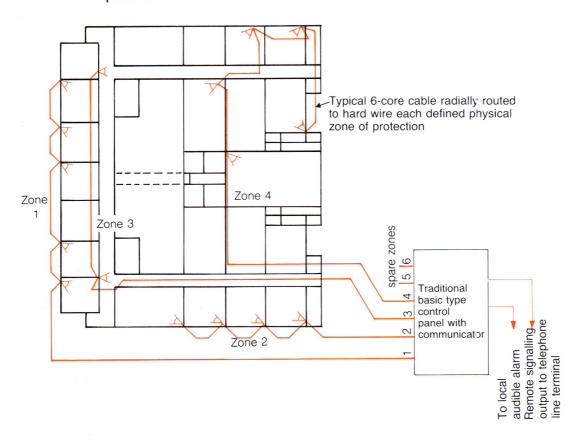

Typical 6-core cable radially routed to hard wire each defined physical zone of protection

Zone 1

Zone 3

Zone 4

Zone 2

spare zones

6 5 4 3 2 1

Traditional basic type control panel with communicator

To local audible alarm

Remote signalling output to telephone line terminal

Fig. 21 Example of a typical wiring system used with microprocessor based controls.

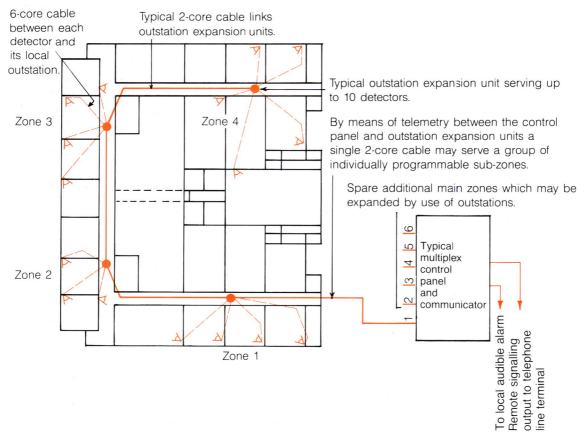

6-core cable between each detector and its local outstation.

Typical 2-core cable links outstation expansion units.

Zone 3

Zone 4

Zone 2

Zone 1

Typical outstation expansion unit serving up to 10 detectors.

By means of telemetry between the control panel and outstation expansion units a single 2-core cable may serve a group of individually programmable sub-zones.

Spare additional main zones which may be expanded by use of outstations.

6 5 4 3 2 1

Typical multiplex control panel and communicator

To local audible alarm

Remote signalling output to telephone line terminal

ability to monitor and report the condition of the control system and any compatible, self monitoring "intelligent" detectors that are connected to the system. Advantageously, a technically deteriorating detector or a near false alarm condition will be reported enabling remedial action to restore security integrity or eliminate a pending false alarm. Condition reporting is through a central station to which the control panel must be dedicated. Therefore the system owner is often tied to the monitoring company's service and its related fees.

304. With keypad operation system access is by the entering of a personal ID code. Unfortunately some LEAs have reported that ID codes have been passed on to unknown numbers of unauthorised persons. Therefore an important aspect of management is to ensure that personal ID numbers are regularly changed and that users are made fully aware of the need for confidentiality. Manufacturers can often incorporate a master key switch if sufficient customer demand exists, but a reasonable user attitude would dispel the need for this requirement.

305. Such is the extent of technical complexity of multiplex, or computer-based, intruder alarm control panels that the purchaser of a system needs access to independent expertise in order to correctly evaluate the technical performance and value for money aspect of systems produced by competing companies.

306. A wide range of proprietary systems of installation have evolved but a generally common feature is the use of telemetry and outstations, to minimise system wiring, and also form a remote point of connection local to the detectors in any area or zone. Generally, the basic multiplex system retains the traditional method of providing separate radial cables to serve each main zone but utilises telemetry and outstations to serve as convenient points of connection for local groups of detector circuits. Individual outstations may be programmed for specific control options, such as 24-hour operation and timed entry/route functions. "Intelligent" systems employing a higher degree of telemetry dispense with the need for hard wiring to each major zone. Instead, normally only one small multi-core cable is radially routed throughout the building to the outstations. Effectively, zoning is achieved by giving each outstation an address reference, that can be individually programmed, from the control panel keypad. The basic programmable options include 24-hour protection, entry/exit route definition and timing and, with more advanced systems, scope for programming various disarm patterns to suit required patterns for partial occupancy.

307. The following list schedules the basic functions typically possessed by a multiplex system. Additionally, the list is extended to include extra features relevant to the condition monitoring and reporting, so-called intelligent controls. The specifier is recommended to carefully compare the operational specification offered by products of competing companies and to also consider the relative long-term cost commitment. With some proprietary systems it may not be possible to competitively tender maintenance and monitoring services.

Multiplex and computer-based systems operational functions should:

■ Comply with BS 4737: Section 4.1

■ Be user friendly and simple to operate by new or temporary staff.

■ Provide keypad operation with option for additional remote keypads

■ Carry log-on codes for authorised persons to set or disarm the system with master code for programming system control parameters.

■ Provide real language display of setting process, programming and alarmed zone identification.

■ Possess an event memory of settings, alarms etc. with memory print out by an optional integral printer or alternatively terminals provided to accept a portable printer.

■ Allow any activation and de-activation times to be selected.

■ Provide control capability to address outstations or individual circuits derived therefrom for programming options. For example entry/exit timer, 24-hour protection and compatibility with local shunt locks. It is recommended that manufacturers' specifications are closely scrutinised to determine the extent of this facility which is so vital to buildings with changing patterns of use. Note: Manufacturers have their own proprietary terminology to describe the term oustation as used herein.

■ Provide a facility for integral or add-on digital communicator.

■ Provide for auto-reset option after alarm condition. (Use of this option usually requires local police agreement.)

■ Provide self-monitoring of microprocessor system and auto-restart optionally available.

■ General features should include: personal attack circuit; timer for delay and duration of local audible alarms; strobe light latching circuits; part set facility; visual indication of live mains supply; audio and visual indication of alarm condition or tamper activation; testing facilities.

- The case control panel and its mounting backplate should be protected with tamper sensitive switches.

- Provide high capability telemetry between control panel and outstations to minimise requirement for hard wiring.

Additional features applicable to computer-based (intelligent) controls

- Whilst an "intelligent" system functions in much the same way as other microprocessor based alarm systems, their computing ability is used to provide various levels of condition reporting upon individual detectors together with the systems functioning as a whole. Similarly, flexible programming can assign a tailored control panel response to fault or alarm signal from any individual detector.

- In conjunction with telephone line communication to a suitably programmed computer located in a central control station, a VDU will inform the station operator of the exact course of action relevant to any fault or alarm signal from any detector. Different responses can be programmed for any assigned detector. This level of central station support may only be available from the company marketing or installing the particular control panel. Accordingly, recurring charges cannot always be competitively tendered.

- Constant system monitoring for fault conditions, with an option for remote control stations to isolate any failed detectors but retain

healthy parts of the system in-operation.

- Automatic monitoring of level of background disturbance occurring at the detectors. Warning issued to control station when disturbance approaches the detector's alarm threshold level. This offers the opportunity for remedial work to eliminate a pending false alarm condition.

- Completely flexible programming of zone groupings enabling any selected detectors to be grouped, or regrouped into chosen zones.

- Double knock option. Initial detector activated and control station alerted. Full alarm is not raised until a second detector is activated. This is a compromise in the level of security but it may greatly reduce the occurrence of false alarms. This should not be needed in a well designed installation.

- Control system should incorporate a powerful event memory. To additionally record operator identification and fault information. These may be time-logged. Option may be available for a print-out of these conditions.

- Facilities may be provided for the interconnection of other building services such as freezer/high temperature alarms, and other plant controls with intelligent information alerted to central control station.

- "Intelligent" control systems are usually developed to work in conjunction with "intelligent" detectors. The specifier should satisfy himself that suitable detectors are available for the particular application for which the security system is being planned.

APPENDIX 5 Alarm signalling – local audible alarms and remote signalling

308. When the control panel is in the alarm status an alarm output signal is provided. This signal can be used to activate a local audible alarm that may typically consist of a bell or siren. Additionally, remote signalling equipment can be activated to use a telephone line to remotely signal the alarm. Usually advice of the alarm is passed on to the police.

309. This appendix describes the various methods for signalling an alarm activation starting with the external audible alarm.

External audible alarms

310. The audible alarm is distinctly recognised as a box, fixed to an external elevation of a building under protection. In order for this unit to be effective the following basic criteria should be met:

■ The housing should be resistant to environmental degradation and constructed to defy the attachment of hooks or ropes or the insertion of expanding foam. Tamper switches should operate if the cover is removed or if the back of the unit is prised from the wall to which it is fixed.

■ The sounder may consist of a conventional bell or a modern two-tone siren but in either case the sound level measured at a distance of 3m, should not be less than 70dB (A). The "sound" should be distinguishable from other types of alarm sounder at the same premises.

■ Rechargeable batteries shall be installed within the sounder housing. Under normal alarm conditions, the control system will power the sounder. When an attack is made upon the external audible alarm or its wiring from the control system, the internal batteries shall be used to power the sounder. A charging circuit shall be capable of restoring the batteries within 24 hrs.

311. In order to comply with the Control of Pollution Act 1974 and the Code of Practice on Noise from Audible Intruder Alarms 1982, it is desirable that a cut-out timer is provided with the facility to mute the sound after a maximum period of 20 minutes operation. Where distinction from other audible alarms is advantageous, a strobe light may be fitted to the housing and may continue to pulse after expiry of the 20 minutes until the controls are reset.

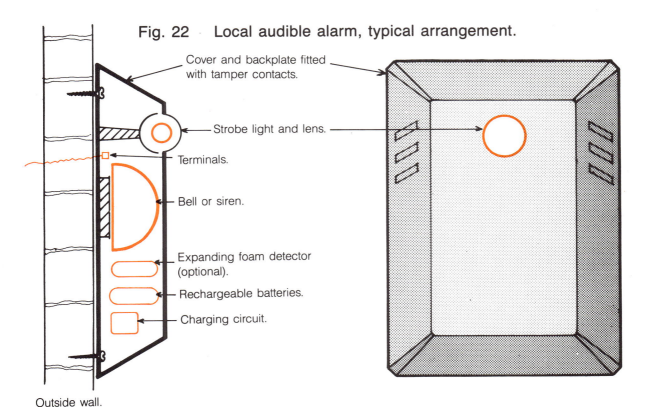

Fig. 22 Local audible alarm, typical arrangement.

Cover and backplate fitted with tamper contacts.

Strobe light and lens.

Terminals.

Bell or siren.

Expanding foam detector (optional).

Rechargeable batteries.

Charging circuit.

Outside wall.

312. The external audible alarm should be securely fixed at a location in a prominent position protected from accidental damage or a deliberate attack. However, attention should be given to ease of access for servicing personnel such that they may perform their tasks within the terms of the Health and Safety at Work Act.

313. Dummy, audible alarm housings may be fitted to all elevations to confuse the intruder and act as a deterrent. Figure 22 shows a typical external audible alarm.

314. Refer to BS 4737: Part 1.

Internal audible alarms

315. An extremely loud, two-tone, type alarm can be effective in disorientating the intruder and encouraging a premature retreat. Ideally, the sound level measured at 3m distance, should be greater than 70dB(A) but less than the threshold of pain of 120dB(A). As a first line of defence the alarm should be fitted with anti-tamper contacts.

316. External audible alarms, with their tamper devices and integral secondary battery pack, may be effectively used in internal environments. Where disturbance to neighbours is unlikely from an internal alarm, the external feature of a 20 minute cut-out may be dispensed with.

317. Refer to BS 4737: Part 1.

Remote signalling apparatus

318. When an intruder is detected, most systems will set off the local audible alarms. The ringing bells would usually alert members of the public who would bring the alarm to the attention of the local police. However, as the number of intruder alarm systems has increased false alarms have become common-place.

319. In many localities local audible alarms cannot be relied upon to reach the attention of the police. The enforcement of the Control of Noise Order restricts the sounding of an alarm to a maximum period of 20 minutes. Buildings within their own grounds or remote from public awareness are particularly vulnerable when reliance is solely placed upon the local audible alarm. To overcome these problems many systems use special equipment to raise a remote alarm.

320. Communication equipment, often in the control panel, utilises a telephone line to alert an alarm activation. Generally this information is routed through to the local police via the British Telecom lines or to a private central control station. Local police forces have intruder alarms policies which entail withdrawal of police response after a predetermined number of false calls, typically four in twelve months. This conserves police manpower and at the same time benefits the owners of reliable well-managed alarm systems since their credibility augurs well for an urgent police response. In respect of this, the transmitted information must be clear and concise, and the police should be regularly updated with correct keyholder details.

321. There are two common types of remote signalling apparatus.

Auto diallers

322. Basic units may be programmed to dial any one telephone number and subsequently play a pre-recorded tape message to the answered telephone.

323. Multi-message units are also available. These will relay the appropriate taped message to any one of three pre-programmed numbers. Usefully, intruder, fire alert, and engineering plant failure can be incorporated. With some auto diallers it is possible to make successive calls such that the school keeper can be alerted immediately after the 999 call.

324. For intruder alarm applications it is most common for the unit to dial "999" and play a taped message to the British Telecom emergency operator. Since the taped message constantly repeats itself it may be simply connected to the local police control room. From here the police will usually issue a radio message to the nearest available patrol car. It is essential that all such equipment be connected with the prior agreement of the local police, since requirements can vary from one area to another.

325. Where the telephone line used is that of the normal occupants it is recommended for the British Telecom change-over switch to be fitted adjacent to the alarm control panel. It is also useful to provide a telephone line testing socket at that location.

Auto diallers – operational requirements

- Reliability. These units contain both electrical and mechanical components that must work, first time, and every time an alarm condition occurs. They are not self-monitoring and regular testing is essential. The unit should be manufactured to a very high standard and approved by British Telecom or other relevant telecommunication authority. Older models are often claimed to be unreliable.

- Contingency alarm. In the event of the intruder alarm control panel signalling an alarm condition, the occurrence of any of the following shall cause the immediate activation of the local audible alarm: failure of tape message, telephone line fault; or line jammed due to incoming ringing.

- In conjunction with a compatible alarm control panel, a time delay facility may be available for the local audible alarm. This facility should be used with care as delay can give intruders adequate opportunity to steal, cause damage or start a fire and escape before the alarm sounds.

- The unit should incorporate a surge arrestor to protect against the transient effects of lightning, or other induced voltage on the telephone line.

- The unit should be tamper protected.

Digital communicators

326.   Digital communicators are made to be plugged-in and hence incorporated inside compatible control panels or, when in their own enclosure, be positioned adjacent to the intruder alarm control panel. Effectively, they are interconnected between the output of the alarm control panel and the input to a telephone line. When an alarm is activated, the digital communicator's output locks onto the telephone line and waits a few moments for acknowledgement of the dialling tone. Automatically, a pre-programmed telephone number is signalled. The public telephone network makes contact to a central station receiver whereupon the receiver returns an acknowledgement signal confirming to the communicator a successful connection. The communicator then releases a customer code followed by an appropriate alarm code. The customer's premises is identified and the alarm code is translated at the control station to enable the operator to take the appropriate course of action. Typically, digital communicators are capable of transmitting up to eight separate codes which may include such items as alarm status, first and second knock conditions, system open time, system closed time and other signals including those relating to the fire alarm or other services. When the full message has been received the central station issues a close down signal enabling the digital communicator to release the telephone line in preparation for a future activation. If the communication link fails, the digital communicator should make at least two more dialling attempts. After which some digital communicators can pursue communication on an alternative pre-programmed telephone number. An output should be provided to instigate an immediate local audible alarm if communications cannot be established during an alarm activation. Often in conjunction with a compatible alarm control panel, a time delay may be available for the external local audible alarm circuit. The digital communicator should be capable of on site re-programming such that it is simple to change to an alternative monitoring service telephone number.

327.   For applications where an exclusive telephone line is not provided, connections to the digital communicator should be arranged to be capable of permitting use of the telephone without activating an audible fault condition during unarmed periods of occupancy. A visual indicator on the control panel should indicate the apparent loss of telephone line. It is imperative that the digital communicator always functions correctly under an activation signal. In respect of this regular testing and maintenance is essential.

328.   In conjunction with computer based control panels, it should be possible to programme an auto-test between the digital communicator and central station receiver to periodically monitor the integrity of the communicator's transmitter and its associated telephone line. This is a feature that should be used with care to avoid high telephone call charges. It is extremely important that digital communicators are fully compatible with the central station receiver. In respect of this the technical specification should be examined in preference to manufacturers' sales literature. With the advent of more digital telephone exchanges there is greater scope to make use of fast format digital communicators.

329.   Unlike the 999 auto dialler, digital communicators must be used in conjunction with a central station and the subsequent additional costs should be considered in viability studies.

Remote signalling communication medium

330.   Communications should be viewed as an all-embracing concept. Accordingly, the choices between auto-dialling, digital communication or direct line continuous computerised monitoring should be taken together with the type of telephone line to be used. Telephone lines are vulnerable at a point where they enter a building. Greater security exists when they are run underground to emerge inside the protected building.

Basic exchange lines

331. This low cost method utilises the normal subscriber's telephone line that is "switched over" to the alarm system during periods of unoccupancy when the alarm is in the active mode. The necessary alteration to an existing telephone is simple and it is effected for a moderate charge. Auto-diallers and digital communicators may utilise this method of communication. Line faults, telephone traffic congestion and deliberate "ringing in" by third parties may disable the alarm transmission. An improvement upon this is afforded by an exclusive, ex-directory line barred for incoming calls, which eliminates the disabling effect of "ringing in". However, this line will attract its own separate telephone line account charges.

332. Where more than one telephone line enters the school it may be possible to designate one line as an outgoing calls only line. It could be used for normal calls during the working day and switched to the alarm system at other times.

Scan monitored exchange line

333. At the protected premises the normal telephone line is permanently interfaced with a small electronic outstation of a mainstation monitoring scanner located in the local telephone exchange. The subscriber may make full normal use of the telephone whilst the scanner silently checks the status of the alarm system and telephone line continuity. In the event of a line fault or alarm condition, the occurrence is electronically reported fron the local telephone exchange by high integrity duplicated private lines to a secure computer installation located within the telephone network. From here, similar high security private telephone lines interconnect with a compatible, privately owned, computerised central control station. Normally the central control station will be owned by one of the national alarm companies whose computerised monitoring will display the appropriate action to be followed in any alarm or alert condition. Usefully, other building services and engineering plant controls may also communicate their status condition.

334. A variant on the above dispenses with the private central control station. A computerised processor in a main telephone exchange will direct the signal to the police or other emergency service. Throughout the system, careful coordination of alarm detectors and their related signals is essential to ensure that appropriate alerts are directed to the correct emergency service. Naturally, the police are only interested in genuine alarm condition reports

and further status monitoring such as opening, closing and general condition reporting require the services of a private or LEA central monitoring station.

335. Anyone proposing to enter into a contract for a proprietary communication system, as detailed above, must assess the full technical features and the extent of recurring charges. In respect of this, it should be determined whether or not the telephone line charges are incorporated in the recurring charges levied by the monitoring company.

336. By virtue of the fact that the systems described here use the subscriber's ordinary telephone line, scope exists for communications of high security at a reasonable price. Future innovations are likely to increase the scope for adding the monitoring and control of additional building services.

Direct (private) line

337. In most instances this will be the most expensive form of communication medium. A private telephone line is permanently connected to the alarm system. The line is continuously "live" eliminating the requirement for auto or digital dialling.

338. This method of communication is most often employed in high security applications where the private line is directly extended to a distant computerised central control station. Sometimes, the telephone line rental cost may be reduced when it is possible to terminate at a local multiplex interface extended by private long-distance wires that are rented and operated by the owner of the remote central control station. In respect of this, some security companies have set-up their own private wire networks and may include the line costs in their overall monitoring charges. Accordingly, an assessment should be made of telephone line rental savings against any additional monitoring cost charges for the use of the monitoring company's long-distance private lines.

Future communication opportunities

339. Technical advances and greater open competition in the communications sector will widen the options by which intruder alarms may be extended to remote control centres. Furthermore, the full communication potential to remotely monitor and control building services plant is yet to be realised.

340.   Before deciding which communication medium is appropriate for any application a full up-to-the-minute technical appraisal is required together with an assessment of the long-term recurring charges.

341.   All equipment must be compatible with the system to which it is interconnected and accordingly equipment should comply with the requirements of the appropriate communications authority. As obsolete telephone exchange equipment is replaced by microprocessor based systems the scope for advanced monitoring will increase.

APPENDIX 6   Central monitoring stations

342.   When remote signalling equipment is used an alarm signal may be automatically directed by telephone line to a central monitoring station. Computers are invariably used at the central station to translate the alarm signal onto VDU enabling the operator to call the police or take other appropriate action. It is also possible for non-alarm events such as opening and closing times to be monitored. The degree of sophistication is largely a matter of customer choice. Refer to BS 5979: 1987 remote centres for intruder alarm systems.

343.   This appendix describes the technical aspects of central monitoring.

344.   Central stations serve as the nerve centre from where direct contact is made to the police and other respondents to alarm signals. Their data processing power can be used to provide a high level of technical and event monitoring to further improve security. The effectiveness of a central control station depends upon the amount and quality of information transmitted between the protected premises and the central control station. Accordingly, full system compatibility must be ensured for the protected premises, the communication medium, and the required level of central station monitoring. The entire, and often expensive system, is only as good as its weakest link.

Protected premises

345.   It is essential to determine the optimum level of security attainable within cost limits. Local audible alarms with or without a 999 autotape dialler may suffice for low risk, low value premises.

346.   Central control stations offer a wide range of service options. The intruder alarm system should be specifically tailored to the required monitoring services. As a minimum requirement, the system must possess a digital communicator capable of signalling the premises identification code together with an alarm signal in a format compatible with the central station receiver and data processing facilities. "Open" and "close" event signals can almost be regarded as basic essentials. Alarm control panels incorporating a computer based "intelligence", may enable individual detector monitoring and other forms of central station interrogation. These controls may not be used to

full benefit unless interconnected to a central station with the data processing capability of performing all the required levels of system monitoring. In respect of this, there may be a dependency upon a sole monitoring company thereby reducing future options for competitive tendering of monitoring services.

Communication link

347.   Paragraph 330 "Remote Signalling Communication Medium" details the available options. Essentially, the method of communication should be compatible with the required level of security and be capable of carrying the required exchange of data between the alarm control panel and the central monitoring station. In high security applications the data exchanges may be made in a cryptic form thereby imposing greater demands upon the communication medium.

The central control monitoring station

348.   The proprietors of central control monitoring stations are in the competitive business of trying to attract subscribers to occupy spare capacity within their microprocessing facility and multiplexed data links. With careful planning and coordination in the selection of alarm systems and communication links it should be possible to possess the freedom of choice enabling the selection of a relatively low cost monitoring option. Also, LEAs as owners of multiple intruder alarm installations, can successfully operate their own monitoring station based upon a single micro-computer and receiver.

349.   Proprietary central control stations are constructed to meet various approval requirements and are generally located in high security premises of a bunker type of construction.

350.   The number of alarm systems that may be monitored by a single central control station is virtually unlimited, provided that physical space exists to extend computerised processing equipment. These hi-tech environments are virtually paperless and involve the minimum amount of physical effort by the control operator. Generally, the operating staff are engaged in routine monitoring activities, and are employed in sufficient numbers to respond immediately to an alarm

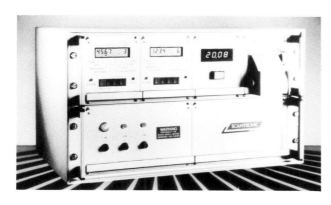

Fig. 23 A typical receiver that may be used to form the basis of a privately owned central station. In conjunction with a microcomputer 3000 alarm system can be monitored.

Fig. 24 A typical monitoring station owned and operated by a medium sized alarm company. Such a station may typically handle up to 10,000 alarm system with scope to expand to 25,000 systems.

Fig. 25 A typical central monitoring station owned and operated by a large national company. Stations like this may handle up to 500,000 alarm systems.

activation. However, every connected alarm system is programmed to have priorities assigned to different alarm conditions and a computerised queuing system ensures that during exceptionally busy periods events such as personal attacks and intruder detection take preference over events such as "late to close" signals.

351.   In response to a data transmission from the protected premises alarm system, the central control station's computer produces a real language display upon the operator's VDU. The displayed text instructs the operator on his course of action and details telephone numbers to alert the local police and relevant keyholders. Optionally, these telephone numbers may be dialled automatically to conserve the operator's time. By carrying out a simple keyboard operation the operator is required to log and record his actions. Where expanded monitoring options are utilised, fire and plant failure alerts may be advised to the central control station and subsequently relayed to the relevant respondents by telephone.

352.   Where an intruder alarm system condition

monitoring is incorporated, technical information such as near false alarms or detector performance degradation is temporarily stored and reported to the service engineer. Often a hard copy print-out is issued.

353.   By necessity, the *modus operandi* described here is in general terms. Intending users of central stations should ascertain for themselves the compatibility of the services offered to their own alarm system and security needs. Figures 23, 24 and 25 show the range of central station options.

354.   Where owners of multiple intruder alarm installations establish their own monitoring central station, scope exists for the efficient administration of the alarm systems. Optional software enables the monitoring micro-computer to control service visits, raise repair and maintenance orders and further control invoice authorisation. Continued software development is likely to extend this range of administration facilities. A micro-computer with a 40 mega-byte hard disc may handle up to 3,000 separate alarm systems.

GLOSSARY

Hertz (Hz)	SI Unit of frequency. Previously referred to as cycles per second.
Ultrasonic frequency	Frequency of mechanical vibration above the range audible to the human ear.
Doppler effect	Apparent change in frequency of sound, light, or radio waves caused by relative motion between the points of transmission and reception of the radiated waves.
Masking	Disabling of a movement detector by positioning a physical object to shield the detector's sensor or receiver from the intended field of coverage for motion detection.
Reed contacts	Electrical contacts located at the ends of reed like strips of springy metal generally enclosed in a vacuum envelope. Under the influence of magnet, the contacts may make or break contact.
Absolute zero	A theoretical temperature equal to minus $273.15°C$.
Absolute temperature	A scale of temperature measured from absolute zero. Note: $0°C = 273.15K$. A unit degree Celsius is exactly equal to a unit degree Kelvin.
Trap protection	Detectors installed strategically in circulation areas to restrict undetected movement throughout a protected building.
Walk test	Slow walking to establish range of detection. Generally, a light on the detector illuminates when movement is sensed.
Shunt out	Partial disarming of an armed alarm system. Generally provided when occupancy is required to a limited area of a building.
Zone omit units	Proprietary key operated devices to shunt out an alarm circuit.
PIR	Passive infrared detector.
Quad	A term applied to a PIR detector where two, dual element sensors are used to divide each detection zone into four segments.
Multiplex	Electronic circuitry or equipment capable of handling a multiple amount of data.
Fresnel lens	Flat optically worked plastic. Alternative to conventional lenses.
Multi path reception	Signals received from more than one direction, usually as a result of original signal being reflected off physical objects.
Catenary wire	Wire of high tensile strength use to support electric cable between two points of suspension.

Printed in the United Kingdom for Her Majesty's Stationery Office Dd 289052 7/89 C50 398/2 12521